St Anton

A Mad Dog Ski resort guide

First edition 2007
Published by Mad Dog Ski
maddogski.com

Mad Dog Ski
St Anton
First edition 2007

Published by Mad Dog Ski

Design: David Marshall
Printed by: Leycol
Edited by: Tory Dean

ISBN 0-9551215-4-X
ISBN 978-0-9551215-4-8

A catalogue record of this book is available at the British Library.

Contact us:
Mad Dog Ski, PO Box 6321, Bournemouth, BH1 9ED, UK
info@maddogski.com
maddogski.com
+44 (0) 845 054 2906

Contents

About Mad Dog Ski

About St Anton

Planning your trip

On the piste

About Mad Dog guide books; why we write them and how they'll make a difference to your holiday.

About Mad Dog Ski

Not so long ago, my time in the mountains was restricted to one or two precious weeks each winter. I would arrive in resort with my ski buddies, eager to get on the slopes as soon as possible and make the most of every minute there. I won't deny that, as well as wanting to make the most of time on piste, we all partied pretty hard and finding good après-ski spots and somewhere decent to re-fuel at lunchtimes played an important part of the holiday experience.

During my first season as a thirty-something chalet host, I realised I wasn't alone in my quest for reliable information. Week after week guests would ask the same questions; where should they ski, where were the best places to eat and drink, the best mountain restaurants? Mad Dog Ski was born.

Importantly, the information in Mad Dog guide books and on our website, **maddogski.com**, is written by skiers and boarders who actually live and work in the resort about which they are writing. Not only do they know the resort inside out, but they are passionate about helping you get the most out of your holiday from the moment you arrive to the moment you leave. We want you to love the resort and the mountains as much as we do.

With Mad Dog Ski, you can be confident that we will always give you our independent view; sometimes our taste may vary from yours but we only recommend our favourites. Extra special places and people are shown throughout this book as 'Mad Dog favourites'. If you find places we haven't, or have a different view to ours, please write to us or email us at **info@maddogski.com**.

Enjoy the mountain!

Kate Whittaker
Founder, Mad Dog Ski

How to use this book

Mad Dog books are designed to be
used in resort. To keep them small
enough for your ski jacket pocket
we've stuck to just the essentials.
For the full low down on planning
your trip (your travel options, where
to stay and that kind of thing)
check out maddogski.com.

The book has seven key
chapters, giving you the following
information:

About St Anton

An introduction to the resort and
the Arlberg ski area.

Planning your trip

Useful information to help you plan
your holiday, including airport and
station transfers and things you
should book in advance. We also

give accommodation highlights. This is just a brief overview but see **maddogski.com** for more information than you ever knew you needed.

On the piste

Everything you need to get on the mountain as quickly as possible and make the most of it once you're there. This includes recommended day trips showing how best to explore the ski area (and where to stop for lunch and après-ski) as well as our unique Mad Dog piste rankings. You'll also find practical information about lift passes, ski schools and equipment hire.

Food and drink

Independent reviews of our favourite restaurants, bars and nightclubs in St Anton. We've also visited all the mountain restaurants shown on the Arlberg piste map to save you any disappointing meals.

Other things to do

Everything you can do in St Anton when you're not skiing or boarding. From swimming to skating, sledging to shopping…

Children

Useful information including our 'First day at ski school' checklist and recommended restaurants for kids.

The list

Everything else! An A-Z of practical services and resort facilities, including banks, buses, doctors and dentists.

Entries

Whilst every effort has been made to ensure that the contents of this book are accurate, places, prices and opening times change from season to season in ski resorts. We apologise if you spot an error or simply have a different opinion to us – let us know at maddogski.com so that we can update our website.

Signs and symbols

A key for the symbols used throughout the book is included at the beginning of the relevant section.

Maps

The map on page 8 shows the main landmarks we use to guide you about the resort. Restaurants and bars are shown at the beginning of **Food and drink** (page

86) and mountain restaurant maps are on page 116.

Prices

Unless indicated otherwise, prices are based on the 2005/6 season. Prices for food, drink and services in resort are in euro (€).

Skier or boarder?

Throughout this book, 'skiing' and 'skier' are used as interchangeable terms for 'riding' and 'boarder'. No offence is intended – it just seems easier that way.

Telephone numbers

In all chapters apart from **Planning your trip** (page 17) Austrian telephone numbers are shown without international dialling codes.

All numbers are prefixed by the local codes:

St Anton/St Christoph:	05446
Lech/Oberlech/Zürs:	05583
Stuben:	05582

Austrian mobile numbers start with '06'

To call Austria from the UK dial '00 43' and drop the first '0' of the Austrian number. From Austria to the UK, dial '00 44' and omit the first '0' of the UK number.

Although mobiles are as ubiquitous in St Anton as in the UK, you'll find public telephones throughout the resort. Amongst other places, they are at the train station, Post Office and in front of the tourist office. They take either cash or phone cards – the latter can be purchased at the English bookshop (page 143) or the Post Office.

If you're using a UK mobile, check with your network provider that it is activated for international calls before leaving the UK. You pay to receive calls as well as make them, so text messages are a popular way to stay in touch on the mountain.

Resort updates and weather reports

For up-to-date information about the resort, maddogski.com has snow reports, webcams and weekly reports from our St Anton-based researchers. You can also sign up for our useful newsletter.

Tell us about your favourite (or least favourite) places in St Anton at maddogski.com. Simply check out the entry under our 'Mad Dog listings' section and click on 'Write review' or 'Rating'.

We'd love to hear from you; you can contact us by email, post or through our website. Full details are at the front of the book. If you write to us with comments on St Anton, we will add them to our website and include your name in the next edition of this guide. If you don't want your comments reproduced, or your name mentioned, please say so.

About our researchers

Wendy Woo

Wendy learnt to snowboard in St Anton 12 years ago and returns each winter to the Arlberg - her favourite place to ride. As an events manager and copywriter, she has spent extensive time in resorts across Europe and North America. Living between Switzerland and Austria, she runs her own event and communication agency.

Favourite restaurant: Pizza Pomodoro

Favourite après-ski: Taps

Favourite mountain restaurant: Rodelalm

Best piste: anything off-piste!

Hugo Schotman

Hugo is a Dutch ski instructor who works for the Skischool Arlberg in St Anton, in between projects as an internet contractor in Zurich. Currently certified to teach on-and off-piste (Austrian 'Landeslehrer' level and ISIA) he mainly gives private lessons. He has skied in many different places in Europe and also in America.

Favourite restaurant: Underground on the Piste

Favourite après-ski: Anton bar

Favourite mountain restaurant: Mooserwirt

Best piste: Kandahar

St Anton; the inside view of what makes this such a world-class resort.

What you'll find in this chapter...

An internationally-renowned winter sports destination for almost a century, St Anton is a well-established mecca for those who love to combine serious skiing and serious après-ski.

A recipient of the 'Best of the Alps' trademark of excellence, St Anton is one of twelve classic European mountain resorts acclaimed as the ultimate in ski destinations. Lying in the midst of the Arlberg mountain chain in the Austrian region of Tyrol, not only are the region's peaks easily accessible (there's a train station in the centre of the resort), the village offers an attractive mix of Tyrolean culture and excellent modern facilities.

Intermediate and advanced skiers especially will be able to get the very most out of the mountains here. Absolute beginners may struggle at first, although the resort has developed more easy runs in recent years (see page 37).

As with most world-class ski resorts, St Anton doesn't promise you a budget holiday but cost-wise it is at least a step down from many of the major French or Swiss resorts. Reflecting this, there is less glamour on display, but this is more than made up for by the warmth and tradition that the resort offers. Somehow the combination of large numbers of younger visitors and a high percentage of long-term residents gives the resort a bright, alive feeling that some larger, smarter places don't have.

Looking a little closer at the visitors, St Anton is not as saturated with British guests as France; we make up only 20% of the visitors, the remainder being a cosmopolitan mix of Germans, Austrians, Dutch, Scandinavians, North Americans and Russians. This gives a lively international feel to the village although English is spoken in pretty much all hotels, bars and restaurants.

St Anton

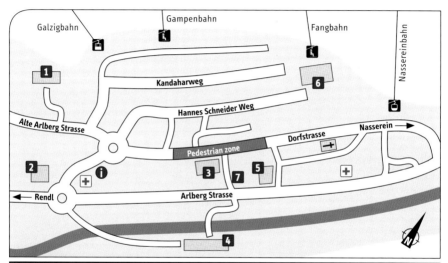

Key:

- ▦ Main shopping area
- ⓘ Tourist office
- ✚ Medical centre

1. Museum
2. Bus terminal west
3. Police station

4. Train station
5. Post office
6. ARLBERG well.com centre

7. Chemist

Getting around: St Anton's main landmarks and areas

- **West end of the village:** central area around Galzigbahn
- **East end of the village:** towards and around the suburb of Nasserein
- **Dorfstrasse:** the village street that runs west to east through the village
- **Pedestrian zone:** the car-free section (*Fussgängerzone*) of Dorfstrasse that runs from Intersport Arlberg, at the west end, down to Café Aquila at the east end. This is where you'll find most of the shops, restaurants and bars
- **Terminal West:** the bus terminal by the roundabout at the west end of the village
- **Terminal East:** the bus terminal near the end of Dorfstrasse at the east end of the village
- **Galzigbahn:** the main lift; at the west end of the village, taking you up to Galzig (2085m)
- **Nassereinbahn:** the Nasserein gondola at the east end of the village, taking you up to Gampen (1850m)
- **Rendl:** the mountain across the valley from Galzig. Reach the gondola via the Rendl Direkt pulley from the centre of the village or a two minute bus ride (Line 1)

The combination of large numbers of younger visitors and a high percentage of long-term residents gives the resort a bright, alive feeling that some larger, smarter places don't have.

The locals are very proud of their heritage and show great hospitality to their guests but, be warned, they do not take too kindly to any bad behaviour, whether physical or verbal!

The busiest times in the resort are Christmas and New Year and then from early February through to early March, when European schools have their half-terms and holidays. The last few years have seen a dramatic rise in the number of people on the slopes due to the increase of beds available in St Anton, extending into Nasserein, St Jakob and Pettneu.

St Anton

Lying at an altitude of 1300m, St Anton is a bustling resort that is very easy to navigate (see map on page 8). Whilst there is no central square, the village extends from west to east along Dorfstrasse (the main street) which starts near the tourist office and runs all the way to the suburb of Nasserein. Sensibly, the central section of Dorfstrasse is pedestrianised (the *Fussgängerzone*) and this is where you'll find the majority of shops, ski-rentals, bars and restaurants. If you're not sidetracked by the shops, the walk from end-to-end will take you less than a quarter of an hour. As you can imagine, this is a very convenient area to stay in, though it can be noisy at night; especially at Christmas when there are fireworks in the street! Not over-commercial, you'll still find enough shops to provide all the retail therapy most people need on holiday. Everything is well signed and you'll soon find your way around.

Even if you're not staying on or near Dorfstrasse, the accommodation at the western or eastern ends of the village (which tends to be cheaper) is well-serviced by a free, frequent bus so you are rarely more than 10 minutes from the centre.

At the far west end of Dorfstrasse, the road takes you towards the Arlberg Pass, St Christoph and eventually to Zurich. There are some chalets at this end of the village, whose prices generally reflect the brisk climb uphill required if you miss the bus (Line 3). Terminal West (where bus routes start and finish) is located near here, along with the main taxi rank (with some of the most expensive taxi-rides outside Tokyo). The train station is also just a few minutes' walk from here, on the main road to the south of Dorfstrasse.

Don't leave St Anton without...

- Spending the morning skiing on Rendl, followed by lunch and volleyball at Rendl Beach (page 125)
- Dancing on the table in your ski boots at the Krazy Kanguruh (page 124)
- Tobogganing down Gampen in the dark, stopping for supper at the rustic Rodelalm (page 98)
- Hiring a guide and heading off-piste or going heli-skiing (pages 35-36)
- Exploring the numerous resorts and villages in the region (page 25)
- Completing the White Ring in Lech (page 76)
- Dining at the Hospiz Alm in the sleepy village of St Christoph (page 94)
- Stripping off and taking a sauna or a steam at the Arlberg well.com centre… or preserve your modesty and swim in their steaming outdoor pools (page 135)
- Staying up till 6am in the resort's nightclubs (page 104)
- Brushing up your on-piste skills at the ski school founded by Hannes Schneider (page 43)
- Being whisked up to Galzig (2085m) on the high-tech Galzigbahn lift, new for the 2006/7 season (www.galzigbahn.at)

St Anton at a glance

- 2,580 residents
- 9,500 beds to be filled
- Access to 270km of pisted slopes
- 180km of deep powder runs
- 38% of pisted runs are blue, 51% red, 11% black
- Some of the best off-piste in Europe
- Four avalanche dogs
- 140 snow-making machines
- Valluga (2811m) is the highest accessible peak
- Season runs from the end of November to the beginning of May
- An average of seven metres of snowfall per season

The village centre

The west end of the village is where you'll find most of the ski-schools and lifts. It is dominated by Galzigbahn ('bahn' means 'lift' in German) which takes you straight up to Galzig (2085m) and the Arlberg mountains beyond. Galizigbahn has been replaced for the 2006/7 season with a new lift that has three times the carrying capacity of the old cable car. Slightly further from the centre of the village is the Gampen chairlift, which heads up the 1850m Gampen peak and then links to the higher point of Kapall (2330m). Rendl's gondola station can also be reached from the centre; via the Rendl Direkt pulley system, near Terminal West.

You'll also find the tourist office at the west end of the resort, tucked away near 'Surfer's Paradise' (a great snowboard shop, page 46). A short way up Alte Arlbergstrasse is the Ski Museum, a few restaurants, and some of the more established hotels and pensions.

After Café Aquila, at the east end of the pedestrian zone, the restriction on cars is lifted. Dorfstrasse then loops around one of the main features in this part of the village, the beautiful Catholic church of St Anton. The Post Office is also near here, set back from Dorfstrasse just past one of the traditional, wooden Tyrolean buildings that now houses a local antiques shop.

Nasserein

Once past the church, a few minutes' walk will bring you to the eastern suburb, Nasserein. Complete with its own gondola (Nassereinbahn) to Gampen, Nasserein was re-developed for the Alpine Ski World Masters in 2001, and still retains the competition finishing building. There's a great beginners' slope here and the main complex houses equipment hire outlets, shops, restaurants and a popular après-ski bar; the Fanghouse (page 109). Bus Terminal East is located nearby. The residential area of Nasserein (served by bus Line 4) has many chalets run by UK tour operators. Even though they're only a short walk from the centre, they tend to

If you're an intermediate looking to improve, and perhaps start some serious off-piste, St Anton is a dream come true. It has enough challenging areas to really push you, as well as more mellow options for easy days.

be reasonably priced. It's a convenient place to stay, particularly as Nassereinbahn takes you directly to Gampen every morning.

An alternative route to Nasserein from the village centre is along the slightly elevated footpath that runs parallel to the main street. When the snow coverage isn't too heavy, you'll see numerous modern sculptures along the trail, which also takes you past the wonderfully modern and well-equipped

Arlberg-well.com sports centre (page 135) complete with ice-rink and outdoor swimming pool. Almost opposite the centre is the original railway station, now a restaurant serving local dishes (page 101).

St Jakob

Next to Nasserein is the peaceful suburb of St Jakob. There are quite a few chalets here, often in more traditional houses and farms, complete with original wooden

features, painted religious figures on exterior walls and even animals in the sheds below (don't worry, they won't disturb your sleep). The furthest part of St Jakob is a brisk 20-minute walk from the centre of St Anton but the bus (Line 2) means you won't be too cut off from the action or the slopes. The main road to the east takes you towards the villages of Pettneu, Flirsch, Landeck and eventually Innsbruck.

Ski area overview

Your lift pass gives you access to the entire Arlberg region, connecting St Anton with the neighbouring resorts of St Christoph, Stuben, Zürs, Lech, Sonnenkopf and Pettneu. With elevations of 1300-2811m, and

more than 270km of well-prepared ski slopes and 180km of deep powder runs, the Arlberg is a skier's paradise whether you like moguls, powder, piste or backcountry touring. A superb network of 86 mountain railways, cable cars, chairlifts and T-bars enable you to travel across the high mountain ranges ensuring even the most demanding skier never gets bored. And, if the lift system doesn't satisfy you, heli-skiing is also an option.

If you're new to skiing and heli-skiing is the last thing on your list, then St Anton can be a challenging place to learn. Having said that, there are some good places to go and it's definitely rewarding (for suggestions see page 37). For

skiers with a little more experience, the lack of consistency with the classification of pistes can be frustrating; what is marked as a blue can feel more like a red and some reds are as steep as black runs. To help you get around this, we have classified all the pisted runs in the resort using our unique piste ranking system (page 48).

If you're an intermediate looking to improve, and perhaps start some serious off-piste, St Anton is a dream come true. It has enough challenging areas to really push you, as well as more mellow options for easy days. The ski routes, which are recognised but ungroomed runs (page 33), are a good way of building up your confidence before heading off-piste.

15

December and January tend to be the coldest months with deep blue skies and strong winter sun amongst the days of snowfall. February and March, whilst warmer, usually continue to provide great snow conditions, as the multitude of north-facing slopes keep their base intact for the season. Sunnier south-facing pistes are kept in good shape by 140 snow cannons.

At the end of the day, whatever the conditions on the piste, St Anton is rightly famous for its lively après-ski, which starts surprisingly early on the home-runs into the resort and continues into the early hours in the various bars and clubs down in the village. See page 105 for our favourite places.

Hannes Schneider (1890-1955)

The son of a local cheese-maker, Hannes Schneider was born in the tiny village of Stuben, near St Anton. As an adult he developed the famous 'Arlberg technique' that became the globally accepted method of ski instruction and established him as the founder of the modern-day ski school. Many people credit him with turning skiing into an accessible sport, rather than just a means of transport in difficult weather conditions. The Skischule Arlberg, established by Schneider in 1921, is still prominent in St Anton (the instructors are easy to spot on the mountain in their blue and yellow uniform).

Schneider left Austria after Hitler's occupation of the country, and moved to the States where he continued to teach and influence skiing techniques across the world. He died there at the age of 65.

It's well worth visiting the Ski Museum (page 140) for more information about Schneider and his wide-ranging influence. The Albona mountain restaurant in Stuben (page 127) also has more detail about his life and works.

Helping you to
plan your trip,
with information on how to get to St Anton and where to stay.

In this chapter you'll find a useful overview to help you plan your holiday including how to get to St Anton and where to stay when you get there.

Our books are designed to be used in resort and so this chapter carries an overview and the bare essentials you might need when you're there. Use **maddogski.com** for all the latest information and more detail.

Check out **maddogski.com**:
- A full range of travel options to St Anton as well as contact details for travel companies, helpful advice on travelling and up-to-date flight routes
- Accommodation advice including reviews and contact details for a range of places to stay
- A listings facility allowing you to narrow your search down and find the information you need quickly
- Advice on all aspects of booking your trip from insurance to the latest snow reports straight from resort

St Anton is conveniently located close to three airports – Innsbruck, Friedrichshafen (in Germany) and Zurich (in Switzerland).

The resort has a train station in the centre, so you won't have to hire a car but can simply hop on the train.

Innsbruck is the closest airport to the resort, having a transfer time of about an hour by road (slightly more by train). British Airways are now operating flights there from London, making it more accessible to skiers. Friedrichshafen is next in line with a road transfer time of around one-and-a-half hours. If you've organised your own weekend trip then Loacker Tours offer a weekend shuttle direct to the Arlberg from Friedrichshafen, with buses timed to coincide with Ryan Air flights. Zurich, although further away, is still accessible as the train transfer is a reasonable three hours (with only one change if you're clever about it!). Finally, Munich is a three hour drive away.

St Anton is a compact resort so you don't really need a car while you are there. However, if you'd rather

Airport transfer times – for airlines, see maddogski.com			
Airport	**Kilometres to St Anton**	**Approximate transfer time time by road**	**Approximate transfer time by train**
Innsbruck	106km	1 hour	1.5 hours (direct or 1 change)
Friedrichshafen	130km	1.5 hours	3 hours (1 to 3 changes)
Zurich	200km	2.5 hours	3 hours (1 or 2 changes)
Munich	227km	3 hours	4 hours (1 to 3 changes)

drive, then you can hire a car at any of the airports (remember to ask for snow chains). If you're happy to go by train, then the service is generally reliable although do make sure that you check the relevant websites (page 22) to limit the number of changes you need to make. Other forms of transfer include private transfer companies and taxis. Details are on pages 22 and 169.

Where to stay

In line with its easy-going approach, St Anton can provide pretty much any type of accommodation that you want. For visitors from the UK, all-inclusive holidays are popular and tour operators book properties across the price range so they can be a wise option for hassle-free planning. For details of companies' portfolios and contacts see maddogski.com. Details of those which are particularly good for children are on page 148.

There is a wide selection of accommodation in the centre of the village (sometimes referred to as 'Dorf' on websites). Nasserein is also a popular area, particularly for chalets run by UK tour operators, and is a fairly convenient base from which to access both the mountain and après-ski on offer. St Jakob is further away from the village centre and therefore offers a quieter skiing holiday, with a short bus commute to the slopes. There are also a number of chalets at the far western end of the village (near Alte Arlbergstrasse). Although these are served by bus Line 3, they do feel more remote and walking into town in the evenings is a bit of a hike.

Hotel-wise, the most expensive options are clustered in the centre of the resort. One of the oldest is the Schwarzer Adler which has a wonderful swimming pool and spa (www.schwarzeradler.com). The Hotel Alte Post (www.hotel-alte-post.at) is also in the centre, and has a cosy, traditional feel with friendly staff.

Perhaps more interesting though are the mid-range hotels, which are housed in some of the most innovative and modern buildings in the resort. Aparthotel Anton is one of our favourites (www.anton-aparthotel.com).

Located right next to Galzigbahn, you won't have to commute far to get on the mountain. And in the evening, the hotel has a great après-ski bar and restaurant, not to mention a compact little sauna area and excellent masseuse. Rates are reasonable, including good deals for single rooms.

Close to Aparthotel Anton you'll find Skihotel Galzig (www.skihotelgalzig.at) another medium-sized hotel convenient for the slopes. There is a relaxed spa area for guests to use, along with a private bar and sitting room. Further away from the village centre, but still an interesting option, is the Hotel Lux Alpinae (www.luxalpinae.at) a dramatic hotel built into the cliff face.

If you are looking for budget accommodation in a guesthouse, or prefer to self-cater, then the easy-to-use tourist office website has numerous suggestions (www.stantonamarlberg.com). They also have details of Hotel-Garni, which are smaller, more informal hotels that you will see dotted around the resort.

Just one word of warning about accommodation in St Anton. Wherever you stay, you are likely to be subjected to the 'Austrian double', which is essentially a double-bed base topped with two single mattresses. We couldn't find a convincing explanation for this tradition – let us know if you do!

For more details and up-to-date prices, check out **maddogski.com**

Useful numbers and websites

In this chapter, UK telephone numbers are shown with no international dialling code (from abroad, dial '+ 44' and drop the first '0' of the number). European numbers are shown with their country dialling code.

Airports

Friedrichshafen:
W: www.fly-away.de
T: + 49 (0)7541 28401

Innsbruck:
W: www.innsbruck-airport.com
T: + 43 (0)512 225250

Zurich:
W: www.zurich-airport.com
T: + 41 (0)43 816 2211

Airlines

Austrian Airlines:
W: www.aua.com
T: 020 7766 0300

British Airways:
W: www.ba.com
T: 0870 850 9850

Lufthansa:
W: www.lufthansa.com
T: 0870 8377 747

Ryan Air:
W: www.ryanair.com
T: 0871 246000

Swiss Air:
W: www.swiss.com
T: 0845 601 0956

Trains

Austrian Rail:
W: www.oebb.at

German Rail:
W: www.bahn.de

Swiss Rail:
W: www.sbb.ch

Car hire

Alamo:
W: www.alamo.co.uk
T: 0870 400 4562

Avis:
W: www.avis.co.uk
T: 0844 581 0147

Budget:
W: www.budget.co.uk
T: 0844 581 2231 (does not operate from Friedrichshafen)

Easycar:
W: www.easycar.co.uk
T: 08710 500 444

Europcar:
W: www.europcar.co.uk
T: 0845 758 5375

Hertz:
W: www.hertz.co.uk
T: 0870 844 8844

Holiday Autos:
W: www.holidayautos.co.uk
T: 0870 400 5561

For details of where to hire a car in St Anton, see page 163.

Private transfers

Arlberg Express:
W: www.arlbergexpress.com
T: + 43 (0)5583 2000 (from Zurich)

Loacker Tours:
W: www.airport-bus.at
T: + 43 (0)664 518 7040 (from Friedrichshafen and Zurich)

Ski Hoppa:
W: http://ski.resorthoppa.com
T: 0871 855 1101

Self-drive advice
RAC Route Planner:
W: www.rac.co.uk

Driving abroad advice:
W: www.drivingabroad.co.uk
Parking information is on page 163.

Insurance
Insure and go:
W: www.insureandgo.com
T: 0870 901 3674

Ski Club of Great Britain:
W: www.skiclub.co.uk
T: 0845 601 9422

Ski Insurance:
W: www.ski-insurance.co.uk
T: 0870 755 6101

It is important to check with your insurance company what skiing activities they will cover. For instance, some companies regard St Anton's unpisted runs (ski routes) as off-piste.

Tourist office
St Anton tourist office:
W: www.stantonamarlberg.com
T: + 43 (0)5446 22690

This chapter gets you **on the piste** and around the mountain as quickly as possible – after all, it's why you're here.

What you'll find in this chapter...

VALLUGA

The Arlberg ski area

Tyrol lies to the east and includes St Anton and St Christoph. To the west lies Vorarlberg, encompassing Stuben, Lech, Zürs, Oberlech and Sonnenkopf.

Open from the third week of November until the beginning of May, St Anton receives around seven metres of snow annually. Your lift pass may seem expensive at first - an adult pass for six days costs €194 in high season - but considering the terrain you can cover it isn't a bad deal. The 86 ski lifts allow you to explore 270km of pisted runs and 174km of powder runs. Almost as impressive are the excellent mountain restaurants in the region. Our reviews (page 115) help you choose the best places to refuel.

Welcome to St Anton am Arlberg! Before you ask, the Arlberg comprises the two regions of Tyrol and Vorarlberg and is a sweeping expanse of slopes, perfect for both piste and off-piste skiing.

St Anton (1300m)

The natural centre of the Arlberg, St Anton is set in the heart of the mountain range, at the base of the Kapall peak. It is brilliantly located for access to the whole of the ski area and has plenty of accommodation and wining-and-dining opportunities for its visitors.

The main lift is Galzigbahn (replaced for the 2006/7 season by a new lift consisting of 28 cabins, each holding up to 24 people) which leaves from the centre of the village, near the fantastic Anton café (page 87). It deposits you at Galzig, where a network of pistes of all levels await. Alternatively, if you prefer to gain altitude as quickly as possible, from Galzig you can take another cable car (Valluga I) up to Vallugagrat (2650m).

The other main lift up from the village is Nassereinbahn, at the eastern end of the resort. This takes you to Gampen, from where you can continue upwards to Kapall, or across towards Galzig.

Generally, expect busy slopes and extensive queues at all of the cable car stations, especially at the beginning of the week when skiers stick close to the village pistes around Gampen, Kapall, Galzig and Nasserein as they try to find their bearings. Hopefully, the new Galzigbahn lift (with a capacity of 2,200 passengers an hour) will help reduce the congestion. A good alternative on the first day of your holiday is to head over to Rendl, where it is often surprisingly peaceful early in the week. To reach the 70s-style Rendl cable car, take the Rendl Direkt rope pulley from the bus station at the west end of the village or hop on the Line 1 bus from outside the Anton café (the journey only takes

If you like to cover distance, then the Valluga-UlmerHütte-St Anton run is a spectacular 10.2km.

a couple of minutes).

The lifts on Gampen and Galzig have a good track record of staying open even on bad weather days. Most of the slopes around St Anton are sun-traps, but watch out for the 'Happy Valley' home run (1, Zammermoos-St Anton) as it often has flat light. It also gets very busy as people stream back into resort at the end of the day. Valluga, being the highest peak in the Arlberg at 2811m, is usually

closed on bad weather days but if you can catch it in sunny weather you'll get a stunning the view of the Vorarlberg and Tyrolean peaks.

When the weather is good, Rendl is a popular choice. As well as skiing for all levels, and a couple of good restaurants (page 125) it has a speed check and slalom run which can be fun (or competitive, depending on your viewpoint). As with all the top peaks, its high reaches can get clouded-out, so watch for weather changes in the deep winter months and keep to the lower slopes. Even when the rest of the resort is closed, Rendl's lower pistes tend to be open.

If you are an experienced skier looking for a challenge, the most demanding runs are on the

steep slopes of Schindler Kar, **2 (Kandahar)** on Galzig and **R2a (Gampberg)** on Rendl. If you like to cover distance, then the Valluga-UlmerHütte-St Anton run is a spectacular 10.2km.

St Christoph (1800m)

Come here for relaxing, cruisy pistes with lovely views over the small village of St Christoph itself. Queues are rare at the main chairlift, which provides quick access to Galzig. Popular with skiers who want to take it easy, or re-discover their ski legs, St Christoph is an enchanting place to be on a sunny morning but when the sun drops behind the mountain range in the afternoon it can get chilly. The gentle skiing, combined

with a lengthy lunch at the Hospiz Alm (page 94) makes it a good place to head early on in your holiday. The area isn't great in bad visibility because it's so open and mainly above the tree-line.

The village is 6km west of St Anton, along the Arlberg Pass. You can either catch a bus or ski direct from Galzig via **8 (St Christoph)**. The last bus back to St Anton from St Christoph is at around 5.30pm.

Popular with skiers who want to take it easy, or re-discover their ski legs, St Christoph is an enchanting place to be on a sunny morning . Come here for relaxing, cruisy pistes with lovely views over the small village of St Christoph itself.

Stuben (1407m)

Exposed to the elements, Stuben's landscape is better suited to more advanced skiers and off-piste fans – fitting as it's the birthplace of Hannes Schneider (page 16). The upper part of the resort is mostly wind-blown and it's a cold journey on the exposed chairlifts. Be warned that flat light hits lower parts quickly so it's not recommended in poor visibility. It's worth the day trip though; the

village is charming and there are a couple of tasty budget options for lunch (Albona and Albonagratstube, pages 127 and 128).

Stuben is the next village along from St Christoph, 15km west of St Anton along the Arlberg Pass. You can catch a bus or ski from Ulmer Hütte past Alpe Rauz, via 17 (Valfagehr).

Sonnenkopf (1840m)

The pistes of this family-orientated resort, which is situated above the village of Klösterle, are often fairly quiet. It's a particularly good area for moderate skiers who want to enjoy beautiful landscape – open at the top, then enclosed by forests as you ski down. Not all boarders will like it though, as it has more T-bars

Sonnenkopf is a particularly good area for moderate skiers who want to enjoy beautiful landscape – open at the top, then enclosed by forests as you ski down.

than anywhere else in the Arlberg!

Sonnenkopf is 30km northwest of St Anton, on the Arlberg Pass. It's less visited than other areas as the bus connection is complicated; ideally you need to drive or catch a taxi (around €50).

Zürs (1716m)

A smallish village, Zürs offers a quiet alternative to Lech. It has a mixture of easy to moderate pistes and cruisy wide-open slopes, although there are fewer groomed runs than in other areas. The weather can

close in very fast here so stay alert and be sure to take a guide with you on bad-weather days.

You'll find Zürs 20km east of St Anton, along the Flexen Pass. It's best to catch the bus (direction Lech) which takes about 20 minutes. A taxi will cost around €40 or you can ski there from the Lech-side of the mountain.

Lech (1450m) and Oberlech (1660m)

Lech is the most glamorous resort in the area and the best place to go fur-coat or celebrity spotting – sometimes both at the same time. With intermediate skiing, pretty pistes and even heated seats on some chairlifts (Schlegelkopf, Kriegerhorn and Steinmähder) this is a popular, exclusive ski area –

and a great sun trap – with some memorable mountain restaurants; try Kriegeralpe or Palmenalpe (page 131). The downside is the queues, which are often particularly long at the base stations. Lech is famous as part of

the White Ring ski trail (see our day trip on page 76) and has a well-maintained snowpark.

Oberlech is perched right on the piste just above Lech. Hotel Goldener Berg, which is owned by the same company as the Hospiz Alm in St Christoph, is a lively place for a sunny lunch (page 130).

Lech is 25km east of St Anton, just after Zürs on the Flexen Pass. It's well worth a day trip there at some point during your stay. The most popular way to get there is by bus (page 159) which takes about 35 minutes, or if you're in a group you can share a taxi, which will cost around €46.

If you want more detailed information about any of the above resorts, the relevant tourist office

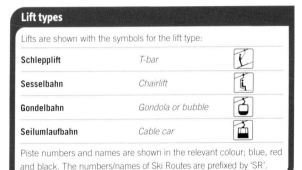

Lift types

Lifts are shown with the symbols for the lift type:

Schlepplift	*T-bar*	
Sesselbahn	*Chairlift*	
Gondelbahn	*Gondola or bubble*	
Seilumlaufbahn	*Cable car*	

Piste numbers and names are shown in the relevant colour; blue, red and black. The numbers/names of Ski Routes are prefixed by 'SR'.

websites are a good place to start (page 170).

The piste map

The Arlberg piste map, available from the tourist office and main lift stations, gives an impressive overview of the whole ski area, from villages at 1300m to peaks at 2811m. It shows the routes and valleys of Lech/Oberlech/Zürs and St Anton/St Christoph/Stuben (including the smaller areas of St Jakob, Pettneu and Klösterle). Of the pisted runs, 38% are categorised as blue/easy, 51% as red/moderate and 11% as black/difficult.

However, the piste map is slightly deceptive in making the different resorts in the ski area look seamlessly interlinked. Although it

With intermediate skiing, pretty pistes and even heated seats on some chairlifts, Lech is a popular, exclusive ski area – and a great sun trap – with some memorable mountain restaurants.

is possible to ski to Zürs from St Anton (via Valluga) the extreme terrain means that you are required to be accompanied by a guide with you. Indeed, if you have skis with you, you won't be allowed on the Valluga II lift without a guide! To get to Zürs and Lech, many people ski to Alpe Rauz, at the bottom of 17 (Valfagehr) and hop on a bus. Our suggested day trips (page 62) and information on buses (page 159) give more details.

Each piste on the map is numbered as well as named and you'll find that some runs tend to be known by their name, others by their number. Lech/Oberlech/Zürs and St Anton/St Christoph each have their own system, both starting with number 1 (this can be a little confusing at times). Pistes in Stuben are prefixed with an 'S', and those on Rendl with an 'R'. The full names of the pistes (which aren't always very catchy) are

shown on the key to the right-hand side of the map.

Once you are on the slopes you'll see that, at regular intervals on both sides of the piste, the markers are topped with round signs showing the piste number. Slopes are regularly groomed, patrolled during the day and protected so far as possible from Alpine dangers, in particular avalanches. Watch out for the helpful signposts at strategic junctions, some of which direct you to mountain restaurants.

Ski routes

Runs marked in red or black dotted lines on the map, with their number shown in a red diamond, are known as ski routes. These runs are unpisted so be prepared to encounter rocks, cornices, icy surfaces, lack of snow and other conditions not normally found on a groomed piste. Opinions about ski routes vary; for early intermediates they can be frustrating as they reduce the number of 'official' slopes available, while for more experienced skiers they're a great way to build up off-piste confidence and technique. Be aware that the difficulty of ski routes varies widely; some are more like regular black runs while others feel very off-piste and isolated. Our piste ranking section on page 48 gives more guidance.

Ski routes are not patrolled or groomed in the same way as normal pistes and therefore the official advice is that following them is only recommended if you have extensive Alpine experience or are with an instructor. Unlike regular pistes, they have just one set of markers running down the centre of the run, which are topped with diamond-shaped signs showing the route number.

Remember that insurance policies vary in their approach to these routes, with some treating them as off-piste. If you intend to use them, it's worth checking with your insurer before you purchase cover, and definitely before you leave on your holiday.

Throughout the book, the names/numbers of ski routes are prefixed with 'SR'.

Boarders

The Arlberg is one of the best locations in the world for freeriders but if you're planning to venture off-piste you should always be accompanied by a guide (page 35) even in seemingly safe areas such as Zürs and Rendl. there are only a few flat areas, so snowboarders can ride pretty much everywhere on piste, depending on their level of competence. If you do have to scoot, it will only be for a short distance. Rendl is particularly good for boarders.

Page 46 gives information on board rental and sales.

Snowparks

Rendl has a small so-called snowpark, although it's usually poorly maintained; you'll see it marked on the piste map near **R7 (Tobel)**. Those used to professional snowparks are likely to be disappointed. Lech's park, near the Schlegelkopf lifts, is better constructed. If you come to the Arlberg, you're better off taking advantage of the amazing mountains and terrain and reserving park riding for resorts that invest in them.

Off-piste, backcountry and heli-skiing

The Arlberg is rightly famous for its impressive and seemingly endless backcountry. It offers an incredible experience that you won't forget. If you're either new to the St Anton area, or to off-piste skiing, you should go with a qualified guide.

The Arlberg is rightly famous for its impressive and endless backcountry.

You can book one through a specialist mountain guide company like Piste to Powder or one the local ski schools (page 42). For more information, check www.pistetopowder.com or call 01661 824318 (in the UK) or 0664 1746282 (in Austria). Piste to Powder organises trips for a variety of levels, from competent and strong skiers who are new to off-piste, through to advanced off-piste experts. If you're planning

any off-piste skiing, make sure you read the information on page 40.

You can arrange heli-skiing through Heliskiing-Arlberg, in Lech/Zürs. You must be an experienced backcountry skier and have a ski guide accompanying you (not included in the cost of the helicopter ride). You can book through either ski school (page 42) or check out www.wucher.at.

Local ski instructor and guide Andy Thurner has written two good reference books for off-piste skiing. Available in both German and English, they contain 3D maps and clear directions. 'Off Piste, All Around the Arlberg' and 'Arlberg Ski Touring Guide' are available in most ski stores.

Off-piste: where to head

The Arlberg offers a vast amount of off-piste from wide open faces to sensational tree skiing. Many areas can be reached from the lifts, although it's often worth a 15-minute hike to find some hidden powder!

The best introduction to off-piste skiing are the ski routes, (marked with red diamonds on the piste maps).

On a powder day the off-piste near the lifts tends to get skied out quickly. However, in areas such as Stuben (well-known for the powder it receives each year) and Rendl, which offers various bowls and numerous challenging routes, untracked powder can still be found many days after a fresh snowfall.

For advanced skiers, a ride on the Valluga II cable car - only accessible with a qualified guide (page 35) - will take you to the Valluga summit, and the famously steep north face leading to the seemingly endless slopes into Zürs.

The Arlberg is also great for ski touring. There are many tours accessible from the lifts, especially from the Rendl and Stuben (Maroiköpfle) areas. However, some entry points can be complicated and it's recommended that you take a guide with you.

If you decide to venture off-piste the minimum equipment that you should take is an avalanche transceiver, a shovel and a probe. It's important that everyone in the group not only has this equipment, but also knows how to use it. A qualified mountain guide is necessary both for your safety and for finding the best snow the Arlberg has to offer.

This information was provided by Piste to Powder mountain guides, www.pistetopowder.com (0664 174 6282).

Mountain Guides
St. Anton – Austria
www.pistetopowder.com
Tel: +43 664 174 6282

Beginner runs and children's areas

If you're a beginner you may notice with some alarm that, unlike the French system, St Anton has no green runs marked on the piste map. Although it's true that St Anton isn't the ideal beginners' resort, there is a choice of gentler slopes, especially the blue pistes around Nasserein and Gampen. 5 (Osthang Einfahrt) is a popular run for beginners. Also good is Rendl, which has slopes for skiers of all standards and a basic snowpark.

The designated beginner areas for children – Kinderpark and Kindlisfeld – are near Nasserein and highlighted on the piste map with a snowman symbol. More information for families, including ski schools and good places to stop for lunch, can be found in the **Children** chapter on page 145.

Cross-country (*Langlauf*)

Although St Anton is not particularly renowned for its cross-country skiing there are a few tracks giving access to over 40km of terrain, with options to suit beginners and experts. The wonderful trail through the Verwall Valley is about 10km long, with a rustic alm conveniently situated half-way along. The Loipe Ganderau takes you round St Jakob and is shorter at 3km. If you're after a challenge try the harder 22km trail to Flirsch. Experienced langlaufers can pick up a trail map at most ski hire outlets, whilst beginners can register for courses at the ski schools. Cross-country equipment can be rented throughout the resort.

Lift passes

- All prices for the Arlberg Card (the standard plastic ski pass) include a refundable charge of €4. To reclaim your €4, simply return your card to a lift pass office at the end of your trip
- The basic ski pass covers the whole of the Arlberg region, as shown on the piste map, although there are exceptions for beginners (see below)
- Men born in 1942 and earlier (1947 and earlier for women) qualify for a discount; €167 for a six-day pass in high season. Those born in 1931 or earlier qualify for a well-deserved 'senior

active' pass for just €10 for the entire season

- If you are buying a discounted pass (eg for senior citizens, children or teenagers) you will need to provide ID showing proof of age (without photo for children up to 1.5m tall)
- Passport photos are generally not needed. The main exception is for passes of 10 days or longer. In addition, if you have a pass valid for six days or more and wish to extend it you will need to take a photo to the lift pass office (on the fourth day of validity at the latest). There is a small charge for extensions
- Lift passes can be bought from 2pm for use the following day. They can be used from 4pm the day before they become valid
- Beginners' tickets can be bought for the practice and baby lifts. A day ticket costs €20.50 for adults and teenagers, €14.50 for children
- A 30-point ticket (between one and five points are deducted each time you use the lift; the back of the piste map provides full details) costs €18 for adults and teenagers, €12.50 for children
- A day pass for Rendl costs €31 (€18.50 for children)

Full details on lift passes can be found at www.skiarlberg.at (go to the 'St Anton' section and select 'ski passes' from the menu on the left-hand side).

Adult lift pass prices (high season) for 2006/7 season

No of days	Cost in €
Half day (from 12pm)	31.00
1	40.50
2	77.00
3	112.00
4	142.00
5	168.00
6	194.00
10	285.00
14	354.00
Season	650.00

For details of cheaper passes for kids see our chapter on 'Children', (page 148).

Although lift passes cannot be purchased online, if you have booked a package holiday your tour operator will usually be able to buy your pass and deliver it to your accommodation, which will save you queuing. Many hotels also offer this service.

Passes are sold at Galzigbahn base station. Opening hours are 8am-4.30pm (later on Saturdays). You can also buy tickets at Nassereinbahn and Rendl.

Lift opening times

Lift opening and closing times vary throughout the season, and also depend on the weather. The first lifts leave at 8.30 or 9am (Galzigbahn, Nassereinbahn and Rendl all start at 8.30am). Lifts tend to close early, usually at around 4pm. Lift stations have up-to-date information or look at 'Latest News' on www.skiarlberg.at.

Other information

Ski and cable car stations both on the mountain and in resort have helpful information boards (and copies of the piste map) letting you know which lifts are open, local temperatures, depth of snow and wind speed. Since information and conditions can change rapidly it's sensible to make a habit of checking these boards, especially when the weather looks like it might close in.

Avalanche!

Whilst every effort is made to prevent avalanches in St Anton, the danger can never be completely averted and every year people are injured or die on the mountain. Sadly, the 2005/6 season saw a particularly high death toll in the Alps.

Speed is of the essence if someone is caught in an avalanche; if the victim is alive after the initial impact there is an 80% chance of survival if rescued within 12 minutes, after 15 minutes the probability of a successful rescue drops dramatically. If you're planning to go off-piste, see page 36 for safety advice and details of essential off-piste kit.

The avalanche risk is defined as follows:

 Low

 Moderate

 Considerable

 High

5 Very high

A flashing yellow light displayed on the information boards at cable car stations indicates that there is a level 4 (high) or 5 (very high) risk of avalanche away from the prepared runs. When this happens, it is forbidden by law to enter closed areas.

For details of the current hazard level, what the levels signify and what activity is appropriate in the conditions, see www.skiarlberg.at – under St Anton go to 'Latest News' and then 'Avalanche'.

Information can be obtained from the Tyrolean Avalanche Warning Service, 0800 800 503, www.lawine.at (German only). The tourist office and ski schools also have local information about avalanches. Arlberg Avalanche Camps are planned for the 2006/7 season to raise awareness about potential risks.

Safety

Most accidents on the slopes are caused by collisions; in good conditions, it is relatively easy for adult skiers to achieve speeds of over 50kph; even children can quite easily reach 45kph. Be aware of others and make sure you follow the rules of the piste shown here.

When the sun is shining and the pistes are freshly groomed it can be easy to forget that skiing and snowboarding are dangerous sports.

Rules of the piste

1. Check that the bindings on your skis are set correctly

2. Respect – do not endanger or prejudice the safety of others

3. Control – ski in control, adapting your speed and manner to ability, conditions and traffic. Give way to slower skiers

4. Choice of route – the uphill skier must choose his route so he does not endanger the skiers below

5. Overtaking – always leave sufficient space for the overtaken skier

6. Entering and starting a run – look both up and down the piste before you head off

7. Stopping on the piste – avoid stopping at narrow or low visibility areas. Always stop at the edge of the piste rather than in the middle and make sure that you can be easily seen by approaching skiers

8. Climbing – if you have to walk up or down the piste, do so at the edge and ensure neither you nor your equipment are a danger to anyone else

9. Signs and markings – respect the information given about pistes and the weather

Emergency piste telephone numbers

These numbers are given on the piste map and listed on the inside front cover. We advise programming them into your mobile phone at the start of your holiday and always carrying a piste map. If you are unlucky enough to need to call piste security, give as much information as possible about the nature of the accident and your location.

Weather

Although somewhat bizarre viewing, the local TV channels provide a good overview of the day's weather. The Panorama-Channel shows live video of various points on the mountains, with temperatures and weather updates. Weather forecasts and snow conditions can also be found at www.skiarlberg.at.

Bad weather days

Cold weather with poor visibility is usually linked to December to February, though March and April can have long days of snow followed by sunny skies.

When the weather is at its worst, the highest lift points are most likely to be closed:
• Valluga I & II
• Schindlergrat, Trittkopf, Kapall, Gampberg, Riffel II, Arlenmähder
• In Oberlech and Lech the Kriegerhorn, Rotschrofen and Steinmeder

The lifts most likely to stay open in bad weather are:
• Galzig, Gampen, Osthang
• In Zürs and Lech, Zürsersee, Seekopf, Hexenboden and Schlegelkopf I & II
• Even when the rest of the resort's slopes are closed, Rendl's lower slopes tend to stay open, so it's a good place to head when the cloud comes down.

Ski and snowboard schools

There are only two ski schools in St Anton - Skischule Arlberg and Skischule St Anton. Although both are now owned by the same company, they maintain separate offices and their instructors can be distinguished by their different uniforms; Skischule Arlberg's kit is blue and yellow, Skischule St Anton tutors wear red and white. Prices and programmes are comparable for both schools, with a vast variety of skiing and boarding courses for all levels of proficiency. Details can be found on the companies' websites. Both schools have good reputations though the Skischule Arlberg is considerably larger and has been around for much longer. Remember to request an English-speaking instructor when booking your lessons.

Skischule Arlberg

The main office is at Kandaharweg 15, opposite the Gampen chairlift, 05446 3411, www.skischool-arlberg.com. Other offices are on the pedestrian zone of Dorfstrasse, *in Nasserein and in St Christoph.*
Number of instructors: around 300 in high season
Private tuition: €145 for two hours (additional skiers €20 each)
Group size: approximately 10 (minimum five)
Group tuition: six days (four hours per day) €213
Children: see page 153

The larger of the two schools in St Anton, Skischule Arlberg was founded in 1921 by Hannes Schneider making it one of the most famous ski schools in the world. Still going strong, it offers a huge range of tuition and classes covering skiing, boarding, park riding, ski touring and cross-country. The school can also arrange heli-skiing guides to accompany you on expeditions. 'Freistil' is the freeride/freestyle part of the school, offering classes for both skiers and boarders.

Skischule St Anton

Kandaharweg 10, near the Well.com centre, 05446 3563, www.skistanton.com.
Number of instructors: around 50 in high season
Price/tuition details: as per Skischule Arlberg above
Children: see page 153

The new kid on the block (founded in 1987) is now owned by the same company as Skischule Arlberg. Though much smaller, it too has a reputation for good quality instruction. As well as standard skiing and boarding classes, the tuition offered includes Alpine guiding, telemark and ski touring. Avalanche training and heli-skiing guides are also available.

If you're staying in one of the other Arlberg resorts, it makes sense to use their local ski schools:

Klösterle
www.sonnenkopf.com

Lech/Oberlech
www.skilech.info

Stuben
www.schischulestuben.com

Zürs
www.skischule-zuers.at

Equipment hire

There are plenty of equipment hire shops both in St Anton centre and the main suburbs. You'll find three main companies; Sport 2000 (Team Jennewein), Alber Sport and Intersport (Pangratz & Ess). Expect all the shops to stock snowboards as well as skis although there are also specialist board shops (page 46). If you rent from one of the shops close to the slopes, you can normally store your skis there overnight.

Most of the hire shops are located on or around the main lift bases at St Anton and Nasserein, no more than five minutes' walk from the piste. The main stores stay open late on Saturdays. All the shops have some English-speaking staff, which makes the process very easy. Prices are standard throughout the resort with only Alber and Sport 2000 offering a top end or 'platinum' range of skis. Choosing your outlet therefore depends on just a few factors. If you come with a tour operator, they often have an arrangement with a particular shop. If there's a group of you it's worth asking if there's a deal that week. Otherwise, it's best to head to the shop that's most convenient for your accommodation. Alternatively, if you are planning on storing your skis overnight, go to one of the shops by the base stations or in the centre of the resort.

Since most guests stay close to the village and the main stores, no one currently offers an equipment delivery service to hotels and chalets.

As with all rental contracts, check the insurance protection against theft or damage before signing.

Alber Sport

Six shops across the resort and one in St Christoph. The main store, Sport Alber, is at Dorfstrasse 15 (in the pedestrian zone) opposite the Sport Hotel, 8am-6pm, 05446 340025, www.sport-alber.com. There are three other outlets in the pedestrian zone and further shops near Galzigbahn and Nassereinbahn base stations, Gampen and St Christoph.

One of the big family-run companies, Alber provides an efficient service from experienced staff. As well as the usual equipment, they also stock cross-country skis, snowbikes, toboggans and skifoxes (a carving machine fitted with a shaped ski). Their main shop has a good range of quality clothing brands, including Arc'teryx jackets and Odlo thermal underwear.

Intersport Arlberg

Six shops in St Anton and one in St Christoph. The main outlet is Dorfstrasse 1, at the start of the pedestrian zone (west end), 8am-6.30pm (8pm on Saturdays), 05446 3453, www.intersport-arlberg.com. The other shops are dotted around the resort; Galzigbahn/Gampen base station, Nassereinbahn, Nasserein village, Rendl Beach, Kirschbaum (opposite the Piccadilly club) and St Christoph.

Offering competitive deals, Intersport Arlberg is another big chain that provides good quality technical ski and board brands. The company collaborates with Skischule Arlberg to provide certain programmes, such as safety workshops, and funsports like snowbiking and skifox. You can hire toboggans at the Nasserein store for the Rodelbahn toboggan run (page 140). There is a good selection of both skiing and everyday clothing available at the main shop.

Skisport Fauner

At the western end of the village, near the tourist office, 8am-7pm,

05446 2413, www.sport-fauner.at.

An established small store, conveniently situated in the centre of the village a short walk from Galzigbahn. Ski and snowboard hire along with toboggans and cross-country skis. The staff are incredibly friendly and provide an easygoing but efficient service.

Ski West

Oberdorf 435, take the road to the museum (Alte Arlbergstrasse) up from the roundabout at the western end of the village. The shop is about 50m up on the left-hand side, 8am-7pm, 05446 2176, www.skiwest.at.

A small shop with a personal service from the owner. Along with a good selection of skis for hire,

they also sell clothing and accessories.

Sport 2000 (Jennewein)

This family-run company owns six shops in St Anton. The main store is Sporthaus Jennewein, at the west end of the village opposite the taxi rank, 8.30am-6pm (later during high season), 05446 2830, www.sport2000rent.at/st-anton. Others can be found near the tourist office, at Galzigbahn and Nassereinbahn base stations and at the top of Galzigbahn.

As part of the Sport 2000 chain, you can expect the best brands and the most innovative technical products on the market. Staff are friendly and give helpful advice if needed. A good selection

of clothes and sunglasses are also available.

Specialist knowledge is extended into the snowboard-only stores; Surfer's Paradise near the tourist office and at Nassereinbahn. See below for details.

Snowboard hire

Most hire shops have a selection of snowboards but these are our favourite specialists:

Surfer's Paradise

Adjacent to the tourist office at the western end of town (also at Nassereinbahn base station), 8am-6.30pm, 05446 283020.

Surfer's Paradise (or SuPa) is part of the Sport 2000/Jennewein group. Snowboard hire and sale

(boards can be tested) plus a good selection of clothing and accessories.

S'no Control
In the pedestrian zone of Dorfstrasse.
Part of Alber Sport. Rental, sales, services and an interesting range of clothes.

Clothing
You'll find technical and outdoor clothing in many of the equipment hire shops listed above. In addition there are a few specialist stores:

North Face
Dorfstrasse 56, towards the east end of the pedestrian zone, 8.30am-7pm.

New for the 2006/7 season, this North Face general store has replaced the Amalis restaurant.

Peak Performance
Dorfstrasse 44, in the pedestrian zone, 8.30am-7pm, 05446 4018.
Refurbished since last season. Offers a wide range of Peak Performance stock.

Sport Pete
Dorfstrasse 17, 8.30am-7pm, 05446 3710.
Also refurbished for the 2006/7 season, this shop is now a concept store for Arc'teryx and Icebreaker. They rent out telemark equipment and, unusually, ski garments.

Piste ranking

It's a common scenario; you are poring over the piste map deciding your plan for the day. You know the standard piste-ranking system but, if you are just beginning to tackle reds, there's nothing worse than attempting a piste that is more black than red. And for more experienced skiers looking for moguls or steeps, the official piste-ranking system is too broad to be really useful. You can only have this in-depth knowledge if you live in the resort and ski all the pistes regularly.

Our researcher Hugo Schotman, who has worked for the Arlberg Ski School and skied in St Anton for several years, has ranked all the pistes (blue, red, black and ski routes) in St Anton, St Christoph and Stuben using a star rating system: * = easier and *** = more challenging.

The pistes and ski routes are ranked relative to each other rather than against similar colour pistes in other guide books. Apart from the gradient and width, there are other factors to bear in mind:

- North or south: north-facing slopes are more inclined to be icy, but keep snow longer
- Traffic: less busy pistes can keep their snow longer but may not be pisted as often
- Grooming: the easier slopes tend to be pisted more frequently than the reds and blacks – some pistes are never groomed at all!
- Weather: has there been recent snowfall? Is it windy?

It is advisable to take an instructor or guide with you on ski routes, particularly on the more difficult ones. See page 33 for further information and safety advice.

Reading the rankings

- Pistes are in numerical order by area (ie St Anton/St Christoph, Rendl and Stuben)
- The name of the piste/route appears in brackets after the number
- Blue pistes are shown first, then red and then black
- Ski routes - also in numerical order - appear after the pistes (page 58)

Pisted runs
St Anton/St Christoph – BLUE PISTES

Piste	Comments	Connecting lifts
1 (Zammermoos-St Anton) ★★	Piste down to the village past the Mooserwirt. There is one narrow, flat passage in the middle that gets very busy and bumpy. There's a traverse off to the left, and a sign for the Krazy Kanguruh just after this section, which is easy to miss so keep your eyes peeled.	Galzig Gampen
4 (Steissbachtal) ★★★	This is the only blue run to the village from Galzig or if you're coming from St Christoph and Stuben. There is one short stretch that is more like a difficult red run. You can side-slide across if needed. Sometimes the sides of the slope offer an alternative with better snow conditions. The lower part of this is known as 'Happy Valley' and is very busy at the end of day, since it's the main route back into resort. Skiers lacking confidence should use this route before 3.30pm, if possible. On warmer days, towards the bottom, the snow can become very bumpy, which is tough on the knees. Keep the speed up at the end to reach the Zammermoos. After that, it's all down hill…	Zammermoos Mattun
5 (Osthang Einfahrt) ★★	Nice slope for warm-up or endless practice runs. Has a mogul trail on the side. At the end of the day make sure you catch the last ride up the Osthang lift or be prepared to walk up or take a very challenging ski route down!	Osthang

Piste	Comments	Connecting lifts
8 (St Christoph) ★★	This is the only proper slope connection to St Christoph. Parts of the run are often windy. It's tough keeping your speed up straight into the wind on the flat trails at the top, which can be a problem for boarders.	St Christoph
8a (Maiensee) ★★	A nice stand-alone practice run in St Christoph. You can choose between steep and not-so-steep descents. There is usually a kids' playground at the bottom.	St Christoph
9 (Schwarze Wand) ★	A gentle connecting road from Osthang to **11 (Arlenmähder)** (direction Stuben) or **4 (Steissbachtal)** (to St Anton). To connect to **Arlenmähder** some walking/skating is required.	
11 (Arlenmähder) ★★	Varied run with one funnel near the bottom. Sometimes a bit bare after windy periods and early in the season.	Arlenmähder
12 (Ulmerhütte) ★★	The end of this slope (which is more of a road) goes up a bit. Keep your speed up to avoid having to walk too far.	
12a (Innere Schweinströge) ★★	Wide but steep connection to the Schindlergrat lift or to **11 (Arlenmähder)**. In the wind this can get a bit bare and icy.	Schindlergrat

Piste	Comments	Connecting lifts
17 (Valfagehr) ★★	A very long run. Together with 14 (Valfagehrjoch), this is the longest consecutive run with the largest vertical drop. Connects to the free bus to Zürs and Lech at Alpe Rauz. Also takes you to Stuben, and back to St Anton with the Valfagehr chair.	Valfagehr Albona I
20 (Stock)★	The starting point for many happy days out! This easy road connects to many slopes and lifts leading to the Galzig part of the mountain: back to St Anton (1, 21, 22, 23) or direction Nasserein (23, 24). Merges with 4 (Steissbachtal) and 1 (Zammermoos-St Anton) at the bottom; careful timing is needed to join and maintain enough speed to get round to the lifts.	Mattun
23 (Plattiwald) ★	Gentle road through the forest. Kids can look out for animals on Hoppl's safari trail. Take care crossing the red slope. There are connections to 24 (Stallmähder-Fang) to Nasserein.	Gampen Mulden Fang
24 (Stallmähder-Fang) ★	Gentle road through the forest to Nasserein. There are connections to 23 (Plattiwald) to St Anton. At the bottom of this run you'll find the practice lifts and kids' playground area of Nasserein.	Nasserein
36 (Fasch) ★★★	The first (short) part of this run is almost red. After that it's a nice varied piste to Gampen mid-station. Alternative: start with 37 (Gstans) – the top part is almost blue – and then connect to this run.	Kapall

Pisted runs
St Anton/St Christoph – RED PISTES

Piste	Comments	Connecting lifts
6 (Seichböden) ★	Gentle red run connecting to the Tanzböden T-bar and **2 (Kandahar-Galzig)**.	Tanzböden
7 (Tanzböden) ★	Manageable red run connecting to the Tanzböden T-bar and **2 (Kandahar-Galzig)**. If you're not careful, you can miss the turn to the T-bar and end up on **2 (Kandahar-Galzig)**.	Tanzböden
13a (Innere Arlenmähder) ★★	Varied red connecting to Arlenmähder. Sometimes rocky.	Arlenmähder
14 (Valfagehrjoch) ★★	From the Schindlergrat lift this curvy 'highway' run leads to the Ulmerhütte restaurant and the connecting runs to Stuben and St Anton. It's a great burn to go from the top of the Schindlergrat chair all the way down to Stuben, picking up **17 (Valfagehr)**.	
19 (Vallugagrat) ★	Leads to the steep Valluga T-bar which takes you to the beginning of two ski routes, SR 15 (Schindlerkar) and SR 16 (Mattunjoch), and **14 (Valfagehrjoch)** – it is usually quicker and easier to take the Schindlergrat lift to get to the latter. For SR 15 and SR 16 a little hike is	Valluga T-bar

Piste	Comments	Connecting lifts
19 (Vallugagrat) (Continued)	required, but this may be preferable to a long wait and cramped ride on the Valluga I lift. The only way back is via the T-bar.	
20a (Hinterer Stock) ★ ★ ★	A challenging slope which you may want to avoid! Often icy, bare and in bad condition. You can take 20 (Stock) instead.	
21 (Grün-St Anton) ★ ★ ★	Nice red slope except for a short steeper bit that is usually icy. Takes you past the Krazy Kanguruh and Taps.	
22 (Platti Standard) ★ ★ ★	Moguls underneath the Gampen chairlift. This run is not always available, especially in the first month of the season.	Gampen
24a (Nasserein) ★ ★	Wide red run to Nasserein. Can be icy.	Nasserein
37 (Gstans) ★ ★	Run with rolling hills down to the Schöngraben T-bar or connecting to 36 (Fasch). Good practice area and one of the first places to catch the sun in the morning.	Schöngraben

Pisted runs
St Anton/St Christoph – BLACK PISTES

Piste	Comments	Connecting lifts
2 (Kandahar-Galzig) ★★	Nice wide black run. Good mogul field on the side.	Zammermoos
10 (Arlensattel) ★★	Decent, not-too-long black. Best connection to the Schindlergrat and Arlenmähder lifts. Can become bare/blown off by the wind. You need to keep your speed up coming off the bottom of the black section and will almost certainly have to sidestep up to the chair.	Schindlergrat
25 (Fang) ★★	Wide run in the direction of Nasserein. Often icy. Takes you past sections of the world championship run.	Fang
35 (Kandahar-Kapall) ★★	A varied, curvy and difficult run. Forms part of the men's downhill competition route. The snow off the top of Kapall is usually good.	

Rendl – BLUE PISTES
Note: all numbers for pistes on Rendl are preceded by 'R'.

Piste	Comments	Connecting lifts
R3 (Übungswiese) ★	Very gentle practice run which is normally in good condition. Next to this run you can find a snowpark including jumps, rails and a speed measurement run.	Übungslift (practice lift)
R4 (Salzböden) ★★★	Interesting blue run. Often has icy patches and rocks/stones on the slope.	Maas
R11 (Riffel 1) ★★	Varied run. Keep your speed up to avoid walking on the long stretch of road. If there's limited snow it can be rocky at the top. Reclassified as a blue (from a red) for the 2006/7 season.	Riffel I
R13 (Wasserloch) ★★	Link from mid-station to the R11 (Riffel 1) run. Reclassified to blue (from a red) for the 2006/7 season.	Riffel I

Rendl – RED PISTES

Piste	Comments	Connecting lifts
R1 (Rendl Talabfahrt) ★★	Long run down to Rendl base station. Mostly easy but contains a few short stretches which are more difficult and tend to get icy – remember that you can always take the gondola down.	Rendl
R2 (Gampberg) ★	Nice curvy red slope to Rendl mid-station.	
R7 (Tobel) ★★	Next to this run there is a giant slalom practice run – if there is fresh snow you can try some powder on the side.	Tobel

Rendl – BLACK PISTES

Piste	Comments	Connecting lifts
R2a (Gampberg) ★	Straight run which can be challenging. Sometimes rocky.	

Stuben – BLUE PISTES

Note: all numbers for pistes on Stuben are preceded by 'S'.

Piste	Comments	Connecting lifts
S1 (Mittelstation-Rauz-Stuben) ★ - ★★	Curvy road down to Stuben base station or to Alpe Rauz, where you can take the Valfagehr lift to St Anton or a free bus to Zürs and Lech. The difficult section is the steeper part before the Valfagehr lift.	Albona I Valfagehr

Stuben – RED PISTES

Piste	Comments	Connecting lifts
S2 (Mittelstation-Passage-Stuben) ★★★	Narrow path with sharp turns through a forested area.	Albona I
S3 (Seelehang) ★★	Nice red with a slight slant. Usually in the shade.	Albona II
S4 (Sonnleiten) ★★	Good red run in a sort of hidden valley. Sometimes bare and rocky.	Albonagrat and rocky.

Ski routes

Ski routes are unpisted runs which aren't patrolled. Throughout this book their number/name is prefixed by 'SR'. See page 33 for guidance and safety advice.

Ski routes
St Anton/St Christoph

Piste	Comments	Connecting lifts
SKI ROUTES ('SR')	**ST ANTON/ST CHRISTOPH**	
SR 3 (Osthang) ★★★	You will usually find BIG moguls on this run and it's steep too. It is right underneath the main Galzig lift and surrounded by forest. Great on powder days. Comes out just above the Mooserwirt.	
SR 4a (Skiweg Taznböden) ★	This is an easy road that leads to the Tanzböden T-bar. This piste, in combination with the lift, offers a good way to get back to Galzig without going through the Steissbachtal Valley.	Tanzböden
SR 11a (Schindlerhänge) ★★	Alternative connection back to St Anton or the Schindlergrat and and Arlenmähder lifts.	

Ski routes
St Anton/St Christoph

Piste	Comments	Connecting lifts
SR 13 **(Pfannenbach)** ★★★	Good run for practising powder (if there is some!). There is a nice variant leading through a gully if you keep to the right when you're skiing down (but only do so when with a guide – it isn't secured against avalanches).	
SR 15 **(Schindlerkar)** ★★	Nice route where moguls are quickly formed. So popular, it practically feels like a piste.	
SR 15a **(Schindlerkar** **Steilhang)** ★★★	Very steep mogul field which is often rocky and icy. Difficult to very difficult. This slope may be closed in the afternoons due to avalanche danger, especially when the weather is warm and sunny.	
SR 16 **(Mattunjoch)** ★★★	A long and exciting route with lots of variety. It's very popular and gets tracked out quickly after fresh snow. Stay to the sides for the best snow. Becomes moguled towards the bottom.	
SR 18 **(Pfannenköpfe)** ★★★	Do not stray to the edge of the cliffs! Most of this route is relatively straightforward but it ends in a very challenging gully. It is classed as 'extreme' on the piste map.	Valfagehr

Piste	Comments	Connecting lifts
SR 33 (Mattun) ★★	A long and exciting route. Again, it is very popular and so tracked out quickly after fresh snow. Joins SR 16 (Mattunjoch).	
SR 34 (Kapall) ★★★	Varied route. Nice for snowboarders. Be careful not to stray away from the markers too much in the top area – watch for the signs with the skull! Much of this area is controlled/prohibited, so it's particularly important to follow the signs.	
SKI ROUTES ('SR')	**RENDL AND STUBEN**	
SR R5 (Wannele) ★★	Long, varied, wide route. Watch out for rocks.	
SR R6 (Riffla) ★	Easy route. When prepared, it's almost a regular red run.	
SR R8 (Maass) ★★	Route through a forested area. Usually rocky.	Maas
SR R12 (Riffelkar) ★	Another easy route that, when prepared, feels closer to a regular run.	

Piste	Comments	Connecting lifts
SR R14 (Riffelscharte) ★★★	Good mogul run. Rocky at the top.	
SR S13 (Albonagrat) ★★	Right next to **S4 (Sonnleiten)**. It's a practice ground for off-piste skiing.	

Mad Dog day trips

Unless stated otherwise, you should start these day trips around 9am. This means you avoid the queues that start to build up from 9.15am at the main lifts. From 9.30am ski schools add extra traffic, and slow things down considerably as they have priority queuing. The days end around 3pm so that you can start your après-ski early, or do some extra skiing on the pistes you particularly liked. Most lifts are closed by 4.15pm, or even earlier when the weather is bad. Keep an eye on the information boards at lift stations for closing times and weather warnings.

Timings are based on the pace of a competent red-run skier in fair conditions and assume average length lift queues. Allow additional time if you ski more slowly or you are skiing during school holidays when lift queues can add up to an hour to the schedule. If you are leaving St Anton to ski to another area, it is better to be less ambitious than to miss the last connecting lift home, which can result in a very expensive taxi fare.

Our researchers have worked hard to make these itineraries as accurate as possible. However, pistes and routes can change from season to season so please make sure you take a copy of the piste map with you in case anything is unclear. It's also worth taking a bus timetable with you when you travel to other resorts.

Day trip 1 – St Anton

This tour takes you from St Anton village to the highest point of the Arlberg (Valluga 2811m) and is highly dependant on favourable weather conditions. This is a gentle day, ideal for warming up ski-legs that haven't been on the slopes for twelve months. It takes in some long blue runs and several reds as well as showing you the breathtaking views from the lookout point at Valluga. Be aware that you can only use the small Valluga II gondola as a foot passenger; if you are carrying skis you must have a guide with you, since skiing unaccompanied in this extreme and difficult terrain is not allowed (see page 32).

The route covers pistes close to the main base of St Anton and shows the most popular runs in the resort. It's easy to get home at almost any point and you don't even have to ski from Vallugagrat unless you want to – simply catch the cable-car straight down to Galzig.

Note - Valluga is usually shut if the weather is bad, so we've also given you an alternative route.

63

Day trip 1 – St Anton

Lifts	Comments
Gampen	Get off at Gampen and ski straight ahead 50m to the next chairlift.
Kapall	At the top, turn right and follow **37 (Gstans)** which links up with **36 (Fasch)** back down to Gampen. From Gampen follow **24 (Stallmähder-Fang)** or alternatively take **24a (Nasserein)**. Both go to Nassereinbahn.
Nassereinbahn	Take this back up to Gampen. Take **20a (Hinterer Stock)**. In icy conditions this can be very challenging as there are plenty of moguls – **20 (Stock)** is a good alternative. Link up to **1 (Zammermoos-St Anton)** and ski to the 4-man chair.
Zammermoos	Exit to the left and follow **5 (Osthang Einfahrt)** down to the Osthang chair. Nice gradient and good condition with plenty of room. Faster skiers might have time to do this run twice.
Osthang	At the top, follow **8 (St Christoph)** behind the Galzig lift station and restaurant down to the pretty village of St Christoph.
Lunch	**Hospiz Alm (page 123, 05446 3625). Aim to arrive before 12pm and leave at around 1pm. After lunch, make the short walk to the 4-man chair.**

Lifts	Comments
St Christoph	Take this to Galzig, from where there are two options, both of which end at the Ulmerhütte restaurant. Option 1 takes you to see the views from the top of Valluga II, as a foot passenger. Option 2 is for those (fairly frequent!) days that Valluga is closed, or if you just want to keep skiing.
	Option 1:
	Exit the St Christoph chairlift and ski down the right side of the piste for approximately 200m to join 8 (St Christoph) to Galzig restaurant/main station.
Valluga I	This takes you to Vallugagrat (2650m). From there take the next gondola.
Valluga II	You can leave your skis at the bottom of the lift as it's only for foot-passengers (unless you have a guide with you; page 32). From the top enjoy the breathtaking views across the region. Return to Vallugagrat, then ski down 19 (Vallugagrat), keeping your speed up as the piste rises at one point, and catch the T-bar.
Valluga	At the top of the T-bar turn right and follow 14 (Valfagehrjoch) to the Ulmerhütte restaurant.

Lifts	Comments
	Option 2:
	Exit the St Christoph chairlift and from Galzig follow the very short **10 (Arlensattel)** which takes you to a flat section before going onto 11 (Arlenmähder) which winds down to reach the 6-man chair.
Arlenmähder	From the top, ski down 12 (Ulmerhütte) leading into 12a (Innere Schweinströge).
Schindlergrat	At the top (Schindler Spitze) ski down **14 (Valfagehrjoch)** to Ulmerhütte.
Break	**Ulmerhütte (page 126). After your break, ski down** 17 (Valfagehr) **to the 6-man chair.**
Valfagehr	From the top, it's then a long run back down to St Anton. Follow 12 (Ulmerhütte) which links into 4 (Steissbachtal or 'Happy Valley'). 1 (Zammermoos-St Anton) runs on from this. You will ski past the Zammermoos (4-man chair) and then keep your eye out for the Krazy Kanguruh sign on the left-hand side. Ski across a track to reach Krazy Kanguruh on the opposite side of the piste. It isn't marked on your piste map but you can see the location on our map on page 116. You'll probably hear it before you see it!

Lifts	Comments
Après-ski	Brave Krazy Kanguruh (page 124) après-ski. You are 500m above the town, and the main way to get down is to ski! If that becomes impossible after a few drinks, bar staff can order you a taxi. If the KK isn't your scene, head back to the village for glühwein on the terrace of Häferl (page 93).

Day trip 2 – Rendl-Stuben

This trip takes you to mountains further afield from the main peaks above St Anton village. Firstly to Rendl; a fun, sunny and less-busy mountain that is becoming more popular each year due to its powder fields, long runs and opportunities to just lie back on a deckchair and sunbathe. This part of our day trip includes some unpisted ski routes, which are marked as dotted lines on your piste map. If you do not have an off-piste expert or guide with you then it's best to avoid these sections. If you are enjoying Rendl – and it's hard not to – then you might choose to spend the whole day exploring the slopes. The number of pistes is limited though, as it's mostly backcountry or ski routes.

In the afternoon head over to one of the most famous mountains in the Arlberg; Stuben. The top of Stuben can get windy but, as the birthplace of Hannes Schneider (page 28), it's a 'must do'. You can either ski back on yourself to St Anton or, if you are tired, catch the yellow Post Bus. There is one every half-hour; pick up a timetable from St Anton tourist office or a ski hire shop.

Note – the piste numbers on Rendl are preceded by R (eg R7). Likewise, on Stuben they are preceded by an S (eg S1). The names of ski routes are prefixed by 'SR'.

Day trip 2 – Rendl-Stuben

Lifts	Comments
Rendl Direkt (pulley rope)	Take the pulley rope/moving escalator from Terminal West (near the taxi rank) and follow the signs to Rendlebahn. Alternatively you can hop on a bus (Line 1) outside the Anton café or at Terminal West. This runs regularly (at least once every 10 minutes) and the journey only takes a few minutes.
Rendlbahn [ ]	After the 10-minute gondola ride, you arrive at Rendl. Leave through the right-hand doors onto Rendl Beach and follow **R4 (Salzböden)** for a pleasant warm-up to the Maas chair.
Mass [ ]	Exit from the left-hand side and ski down 200m to rejoin **R4 (Salzböden)**. Ski about halfway down until you reach the Riffel I chair.
Riffel I [ ]	From the top, there are two options, depending on your level of skiing and the conditions. Both end up at Rendl Beach.
	Option 1:
	If you feel confident with unpisted routes (see opposite page) ski down **R11 (Riffel 1)** to the 2-man chair (Riffel II).

Lifts	Comments
Riffel II 🚡	This takes you up to Riffelscharte (2645m) from where you take SR R14 (Riffelsharte), an unpisted route which, although not very long, is pretty steep and gets mogully and can also be rocky when the snow cover is low. This joins up to SR R12 (Riffelkar) – also unpisted, but generally nicer – and then to **R13 (Wasserloch)**, which takes you back to Rendl Beach.
	Option 2:
	If you don't feel confident skiing itinerary runs, take Riffel I chair and from the top ski a really nice long run by going from **R11 (Riffel 1)** to join **R4 (Salzböden)**. Then catch the Maas chairlift back up and head to Rendl Beach.
Break	**Enjoy a drink in the sun at Rendl Beach (page 125). Leave Rendl station and follow the short route along R7 (Tobel) to the 6-man chair.**
Gampberg 🚡	Get off on the right-hand side and follow **R2 (Gampberg)** down. This leads onto **R1 (Rendl Talabfahrt)** which will take you all the way down to the base station. It's a long fun route.

Lifts	Comments
Bus/walk	The bus stops just by the main Rendlbahn entrance and will take you pretty much directly to the base of Galzigbahn in the village. Alternatively you can walk (7-10 minutes).
Galzigbahn	Take the lift up to the top.
Lunch	**Galzig restaurant. You have a choice of two self-service cafes (page 121) or a sit-down restaurant (Verwall Stube, page 127; 05446 235 2501). After lunch take 6 (Seichböden) to the T-bar.**
Tanzböden	Link into **10 (Arlensattel)**, which is a short stretch that a competent skier can manage, onto **11 (Arlenmähder)** all the way down to the 6-man chair.
Arlenmähder	From the top follow 12 (Ulmerhütte) then 17 (Valfagehr) down past Alpe Rauz (don't ski to the Valfagehr chair but stay on the right-hand side of the piste) to the small village of Stuben (you will see signs) and the 2-man chair. It's a long ski down!
Albona I	Ski down a very short section of S1 (Mittelstation-Rauz-Stuben) to another 2-man chair.
Albona II	Follow **S4 (Sonnleiten)** down to the 2-man chair.

Lifts	Comments
Albonagrat ⛷	Take up to top station and ski back down **S4 (Sonnleiten)** to the intersection with **S3 (Seelehang)**. Then take **S3** down to mid-station.
Après-ski	**Restaurant Albona. After your break ski down to** S1 (Mittelstation-Rauz-Stuben) **to Alpe Rauz. Catch the bus back to St Anton from the main bus stop (see page 162).**

Day trip 3 - St Anton and Zürs

This itinerary will suit skiers who have skied around St Anton and feel more confident about exploring the surrounding areas. The route takes you to Zürs and back again and covers long, wide runs. You feel like you are really travelling and seeing more of the Arlberg.

Day trip 3 - St Anton and Zürs

Lifts	Comments
Nassereinbahn 🚡 **or Gampen** 🚡	Take either lift up to Gampen (depending on which is closest to your accommodation). From there follow **20a (Hinterer Stock)**. This is often icy with lots of moguls – an alternative is 20 (Stock). Feed into 4 (Steissbachtal) to the 4-man chair (Zammermoos).
Zammermoos 🚡	Exit right and follow **10 (Arlensattel)**, joining 11 (Arlenmähder) which takes you all the way down to the 6-man chair.
Arlenmähder 🚡	From the top follow **12 (Ulmerhütte)** then **17 (Valfagehr)** to Alpe Rauz base station. From there, take the free blue ski bus to the second stop in Zürs; it's next to the carpark. The journey takes approximately 10 minutes. When you get off the bus, you'll see the 6-man chairlift opposite you.
Hexenboden 🚡	At the top take **3 (Familienabfahrt)** down to either Zürsersee or Seekopf; both are 4-man chairlifts. With both you cross over the road via the skiable bridge using the pulley if necessary; it's a bit untidy regarding piste layouts on the map but, because you end up in the same place, it isn't really a problem.
Zürsersee 🚡 **or** **Seekopf** 🚡	

Lifts	Comments
Lunch	**At the top of the chairlifts you'll find Seekopf restaurant (page 130, 0664 2187). When you leave the restaurant after lunch, ski slightly to the left and take 11 (Muggengrat-Zürsersee) for around 200m to get to the 2-man chair.**
Muggengrat	From the top, follow 10 (Muggengrat-Täil) all the way down to Zürs. Cross the road to take the cable car.
Trittkopf	Follow 6 (Hübner Hang) that joins to 4 (Skiweg), joining onto 3 (Familienabfahrt) which takes you to the Seekopf chair via the bridge.
Seekopf	Get off to the right and go down 18 (Madlochalm), which goes down to the road. There is a bus stop here to catch the (free) blue bus back to Alpe Rauz, which is the final stop of the bus (the journey takes approximately 10 minutes). The T-bar is right by the bus terminal.
Rauz	At the top, go straight onto the 6-man chair.
Valfagehr	Enjoy the innovative bum-warming seats! From the top follow 12 (Ulmerhütte) to join 4 (Steissbachtal) which joins onto 1 (Zammermoos-St Anton) to take you back into St Anton. you'll pass plenty of après-ski bars on your way home.

Day trip 4 – Lech: The White Ring

A famous, established ski-route for over 50 years, the White Ring takes you from Lech on to Zürs then to Zug and Oberlech.

The original lifts and ski runs of the White Ring still form the backbone of the Lech, Zürs and Arlberg ski area and contain 30

cable-lift systems. The pistes between Lech and Zürs, with their corduroy slopes, are more open and less steep than the valleys of St Anton. All the mountain villages visited have their own character. Since you start at Lech, you will need to catch the Post Bus there from St Anton, which leaves from Terminal West. It's best to catch the

8.35am bus (which arrives at Lech Rüfiplatz, the village square, at 9.10am). At the very least, you should catch the 9.05 bus to arrive in Lech at 9.40. The bus costs €3.60 single/€5.50 return. Exit at the first stop in Lech. If you are in a group and want to share a taxi to Lech, it will cost you around €46.

Day trip 4 – Lech: The White Ring

Lifts	Comments
Rüfikopf 🚠	There are two cable cars running next to each other. Take either one to Rüfikopf (2362m). From there, follow **38a (Steinmännle)** to the T-bar.
Schüttboden 🎿	Exit to the right-hand side and follow **38a (Schüttboden-Zürs)** down to the 6-man chair.
Trittalp 🚡	Get off to the right and take **3a (Hexenboden Direkte)** which links into **3 (Familienabfahrt)** and takes you down to the village of Zürs. You ski over the road on a bridge (there is also a pulley) directly to the Zürsersee chair.
Break	**If you feel like a quick snack or drink then the Milch Bar, to the left of the Zürsersee (4-man chair), is a good choice.**
Zürsersee 🚡	Get off to the right and go over a small flat section to the 2-man chair (you'll see the chairlift directly opposite you on the other mountain face).
Madloch 🚡	Get off to the left-hand side and follow a long run, SR **33 (Madloch-Zug)**. This is unpisted but generally fine for red-level skiers (just quite choppy). Goes down to the tiny village of Zug and the Zugerberg 2-man chair.
Zugerberg 🚡	

Lifts	Comments
Lunch	At the top, head to the Palmenalpe restaurant which has a wonderful view (page 131, 05583 3312).

At the top, head to the Palmenalpe restaurant which has a wonderful view (page 131, 05583 3312).

After lunch, take the pulley back to the piste then follow 34 (Kriegeralpe Oberlech-Lech) all the way past Oberlech and on to the bottom of Lech village. This terrain – the Schlegelkopf – is one of the best open-space areas for you to cruise the piste or enjoy some après-ski before you take the bus home. If you are snowboarding, there are some flatter stretches but not of any real distance.

Be sure to catch the Post Bus back to St Anton as the free blue buses only take you part way. The Post Bus departs from Lech Rüfiplatz (the square where the bus dropped you off in the morning, near the Rüfikopf lift) every 30 minutes. For the 2005/6 season the times were 21 and 51 minutes past the hour, but check an up-to-date timetable to make sure that hasn't changed. The last bus leaves around 5pm. From Zürs, the buses back to St Anton also leave every 30 minutes (currently at 26 and 56 minutes past the hour but again check a current timetable).

After all your hard work on the slopes, you deserve some decent **food and drink.** Here's our inside view on the best places to refuel.

Austrian mountain food has evolved to combat the effect of the altitude and the cold; good, solid fare like dumplings and sausages. The main repertoire centres around different combinations of staple ingredients however, with an open mind things can become more interesting.

Amongst the local favourites you'll find pig's trotters, wiener schnitzel and Bavarian white sausages to name a few. For more details (and translations) of the main choices you are likely to come across, see page 83. Traditional restaurants in the area are often known as an 'alm' or 'stube', which basically means 'rest stop for travellers'. They are normally small, cosy establishments.

Although most of the restaurants, especially those on the mountain, offer predominantly Tyrolean cuisine, if you feel like a change there is a tapas bar (page 90) and a reasonable choice of Italian places (pages 91 and 99) in resort. And, if you are in need of further variety, there is also a Chinese restaurant, next to Häferl café on Dorfstrasse, although it's nothing to write home about.

Vegetarian choice

It will take only a couple of minutes for vegetarians to realise that Austrians love their meat, but there are normally alternatives. If you're struggling, restaurant staff often come up with helpful suggestions; perhaps some spinach dumplings or noodles cooked with cheese. Some of the mountain restaurants - for example Galzig (page 121) and Rendl Beach (page 125) - have good salad bars which can give your meal a boost. Old favourites such as pizza, pasta and cheese fondue are also widely available. Our symbol **V** highlights the few restaurants offering a reasonable vegetarian selection. You may not have a gourmet holiday but you won't starve, either.

On the other hand, if you love your meat, then you're in for a real fleisch-feast. Head to the rustic Rodelalm above the village (page 98), Dorf Stub'n (page 91) or Le Fonti (page 92).

Children

For restaurants that are particularly family-friendly, check out our recommendations on page 155.

Budget meals and take-aways

Price-wise, it's hard to find a meal in St Anton that you can truly class as 'budget'. Hunt around, however, and you won't have to spend a fortune. Pizza restaurants

(Pomodoro and San Antonio, pages 97 and 99) are a good start as are places where the focus is on snacks (for example Tom Dooley's and Funky Chicken, pages 103 and 109). Alternatively, eat where the locals do (Fuhrman Stube, page 92, and S'Wirtshaus am Alten Bahnhof, page 101) – the presentation may be less elaborate and the surroundings less refined, but the food is tasty and filling.

Take-aways are always a cheaper option but choice is limited. During the day, you can buy sandwiches and pastries from Alberger Dorfbackerei (page 87). For pizzas try San Antonio (page 99), for burgers the original 20-year-old Hermann's Burgers near the Nasserein lift. Alternatively try

Imbisstand next to Hax'n Stub'n (page 93) though it shuts by 10pm. For those with late-night munchies, there is a new place to tuck into burgers, hot dogs and burritos up till 2am; Burger Stop on Dorfstrasse (page 90).

Once you're on the mountain, finding cheaper meals becomes even more of a challenge. Prices rise with the altitude so if you're on a budget you may want to head back to resort to eat – or at the very least avoid Lech, where prices really peak. Rendl Beach and Galzig in St Anton (pages 125 and 121) and Albona and Albonagratstube in Stuben (pages 127 and 128) offer good cheaper options. The local fast food joint for skiers is Rauzer Stube, at Alpe

Rauz (page 125). If you like picnicking, you'll find details of food shops on page 142.

Resort restaurants

The majority of places to eat in the village are easily located, lined up along the pedestrian section of Dorfstrasse, and within five minutes' walk of the piste. There are also clusters of restaurants both in Nasserein and winding up the mountain from the roundabout at the western end of the village (handy if you are staying in the suburbs and don't want to walk to the centre). In addition to the places listed, most hotel restaurants are open to the public.

The most popular restaurants become very busy, especially in high

Prices rise with the altitude so if you're on a budget you may want to head back to resort to eat – or at the very least avoid Lech, where prices really peak.

season. Germans and Austrians tend to eat quite early (from about 6pm) but visitors from other countries ensure that restaurants stay busy all night. The reservation system varies from place to place – some restaurants won't accept reservations at all, others will only accept them at certain times of the season. If you are staying in a

chalet, then you (or your chalet host) should try to reserve a table at your chosen restaurant for the staff night off. If you don't speak German, then it may be easier to pop in and reserve the table in person. Even if your knowledge of German is limited, rest assured that most waiters speak some English and many restaurants have an English version of their menus.

Useful tip
Resort restaurants (page 82) and bars (page 104) are listed in alphabetical order. Unlike with mountain restaurants (page 115), we only include details of those places we recommend.

Austrian food and drink:

Bergkäse:	a local mountain cheese. The flavour varies from mild to slightly sharp.
Fondue:	although not strictly an Austrian dish, this is still pretty popular here. A fondue pan, filled with either hot oil (for meat fondue) or a mixture of wine and cheese, is brought to your table. Use your fondue fork to dip either cubes of meat or bread into the pan. It can normally only be ordered for a minimum of two.
Gröstl:	a sort of Austrian fry-up; a mixture of fried potatoes, onions and ham/bacon, sometimes served with an egg on top.
Kaiserschmarrn:	hearty traditional thick chopped pancakes covered in plums, jam, sugar and raisins.
Knödel:	dumplings. These are often served in a clear broth or alternatively as a side dish or main course. Varieties include bacon (speckknödel), cheese (kasknödel) and spinach (spinatknödel). Definitely worth trying, and the meat-free ones are good for vegetarians. A delicious sweet version, germknödel, is filled with jam and sprinkled with cocoa.
Sauerkraut:	cabbage, either red or green. Served as a side dish to most main courses.
Schweinhaxe:	pig's trotters. You can find these at Hax'n Stub'n (page 93) and Rodelalm (page 98). Considered by many to be a delicacy – quite fatty and rich but fantastically tasty.
Soups:	popular in the mountain restaurants. Favourites include barley broth (gerstensuppe), knödel soup (dumplings bobbing in a clear broth) and goulash.

Austrian food and drink:

Spätzle: small pasta dumplings similar in texture to gnocchi, often served with cheese.

Speck: frequently translated as 'bacon', this cured ham is in fact more like Italian prosciutto. You'll come across it in many different dishes, including speckbrot, which is slices of speck laid over rye bread and served with gherkins on a breadboard. An ideal lunch on a sunny day.

Strudel: a flaky pastry casing with a choice of fillings, for example apple (apfelstrudel) or soft cheese (topfenstrudel), which is rolled and baked. Delicious for pudding or as a snack.

Toast: toasted sandwich. Comes with a variety of fillings, often cheese (käse toast), ham or steak.

Vintschger: traditional South Tyrolean black bread.

Wiener schnitzel: breaded and fried fillet of veal or pork. Commonly known as schnitzel.

Würstl: sausages; normally pork but a variety of types are available. Served as a snack with bread and mustard, or with roast potatoes and sauerkraut as a main course.

Drinks

Almdudler: a herbal soft drink, very popular throughout Austria.

Glühwein: mulled red wine.

Stroh rum: comes in a variety of strengths but you'll mainly come across 'Stroh 80' (ie 80° proof). A real warmth-booster when added to hot chocolate.

Our favourite resort restaurants

Alberger Dorfbackerie – page 87.	Welcoming local bakery with small café area
Anton restaurant – page 87.	Reliable, well-priced Austrian and European food with a contemporary twist, right next to Galzigbahn
Ben.Venuto – page 88.	Asian, Japanese and Italian food served in a sweeping upmarket restaurant
Bobo's – page 89.	Enjoy Mexican food in this friendly subterranean venue, then drink cocktails at the bar and listen to live music
Le Fonti – page 92.	Classic Tyrolean restaurant with a surprisingly extensive wine list
Häferl – page 93.	Warm and cosy Austrian tea room in the centre of the village
Hazienda – page 94.	Much-loved wine bar serving international favourites
Hospiz Alm – page 94.	Charming traditional restaurant in the village of St Christoph which is worth the above-average prices
Montjola – page 96.	St Anton's most famous fondue joint
Museum restaurant – page 97.	Dine in front of the fire in the formal restaurant of this beautiful old mansion
Pizza Pomodoro – page 97.	Popular budget pizzeria with daily specials and homemade lasagne
Rodelalm – page 98.	Rustic alm perched on the side of the toboggan slope serving hearty Austrian classics
San Antonio Pizzeria – page 99.	Choose from numerous types of pizza in this friendly local restaurant in Nasserein
Underground on the Piste – page 103.	Good food, board games and music on the edge of the piste

St Anton Restaurants

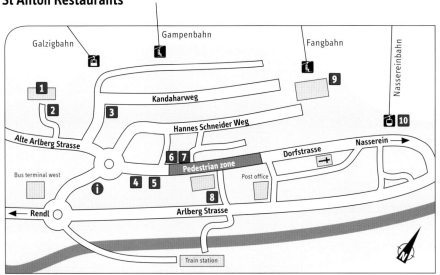

Key:

ℹ️ Tourist office	3. Anton bar/restaurant	6. Platzl
1. Museum restaurant	4. Le Fonti	7. Pizza Pomodoro/
2. Underground on the piste	5. Häferl	Funky chicken

8. Scotty's
9. well.com: Ben.Venuto
10. Fang House

How to read our reviews:

Resort restaurants and bars (page 107) are listed in alphabetical order. Unlike with mountain restaurants (page 121), we only include details of those places we recommend.

 – budget: most main course prices are under €10

 – mid-range: main course prices range from €11-20

 – expensive: most main course prices are €20+

 – reasonable vegetarian choice

 – venues that close late (1am or after)

 – our absolute **Mad Dog** favourites. These are the places that our researchers return to time and time again; sometimes for their classic mountain feel, sometimes for their warm welcome, sometimes for their budget prices and sometimes because they're perfect for a treat.

Restaurants

Alberger Dorfbackerie

Dorfstrasse, on the left-hand side of the road as you head away from the centre of the village towards Nasserein, almost opposite Nah & Frisch supermarket, opening hours vary throughout the season.

The local bakery sells good sandwiches, cakes and other picnic food and has a small café area.

Anton restaurant/café

T: 05446 2408
W: www.anton-aparthotel.com

Kandaharweg 4, at the roundabout near the taxi rank (western end of

the resort), near Galzigbahn and Gampen chairlift, 11am-11pm (earlier for breakfast), reservations essential.

Part of the award-winning Aparthotel Anton complex, this is one of the few contemporary buildings in St Anton, with a strong modern look based on glass and metal. The restaurant and its balcony (with chairs draped in woolly sheep-skins) overlook the village. Food is Austrian and European with a contemporary twist – soup, spaghetti, fondue (in the evening) and Chateaubriand. One of the few places in St Anton to serve Vintschger, traditional South Tyrolean black bread. Attracts a 20-to-30-something clientele. Breakfast

is also served. The restaurant is perched above the Anton café, a small street-level hideaway which is ideal for coffee or fresh juice.

Aquila
T: 05446 2217

Dorfstrasse 62, at the eastern end of the pedestrian zone (on the corner near Bobo's), 6-10pm.

Aquila is more of a café than a restaurant, with a mixed menu of wok dishes (€9.80), schnitzel (€10.40) and vegetable curry (€11.80). The food is reliable, the location convenient and the service quick. A good place to take children because of the simple

options available (nuggets and spaghetti) and the space. Save some room for the cakes! A facelift is planned for the 2006/7 season.

Ben.Venuto
T: 05446 30203
W: www.benvenuto.at

Hannes-Schneider-Weg 2; on the first-floor of the Well.com centre (opposite the old railway station), 6.30pm-midnight, (reservations necessary).

A large, open-plan restaurant, Ben.Venuto is unique in St Anton, offering upmarket Asian, Japanese and Italian dishes prepared in an open-fronted kitchen area. The

cooking is good, with lots of bright, clean flavours including mushroom and guinea fowl risotto (€13.50) and sushi (€16.10). The set menu, offering five courses for €49 (€39 for the vegetarian option), is good value for the quality. Suitable for groups of friends or couples – though a large restaurant, the modern surroundings feel intimate through careful lighting and warm décor. The best tables are by the window overlooking St Anton.

There's also a good wine list (house wine €27).

Bifangalm

T: 05446 30238
    0664 2302220

Rendl mountain, Thursday and Friday nights only, (reservations necessary), transport will be arranged by the restaurant.

Traditional mountain restaurant on Rendl. See page 121.

Bobo's

T: 05446 271454
W: www.bobos.at.

Dorfstrasse 60, towards the eastern end of the pedestrian zone, next to Dorf Stub'n restaurant, 6-11pm (bar open till 1am).

Established over 20 years ago with the Route 66 theme and the 80s vibe is still going strong! Bobo's is a fun place to eat good Mexican-style food and then continue the party at the bar. Dishes include burritos (€11.50), fajitas (€12.90) and shrimp grill (€18.90). There's a variety of entertainment options available: karaoke on Monday and Thursday (the most popular nights with the Brits!) live music (page 106) and resident DJ (Friday and Saturday). The bar gets packed later on.

Bodega

T: 05446 42788

Dorfstrasse, across the street from Hotel Post, 3pm-1am.

Being the only tapas restaurant in town, this compact little place can get uncomfortably crowded inside so arrive early to get a decent table. As you would expect, service tends to slow down with the crowds. Their tapas (ranging from €2.50-9.50) include chorizo, Serrano ham and a good selection of fish. Mixed anti-pasti is €16. Wine is expensive but a wide selection of bottled beers are available. Order at the bar – the food will be brought to your table; the drinks you carry yourself. There's regular live music courtesy of Mexican singer and guitarist Rosella (last season she played on Wednesdays and Thursdays but check the new schedule).

Burger Stop

Dorfstrasse (next to Aquila restaurant and opposite Bar Cuba), 4pm-2am.

A replacement to Snack Attack, which closed at the end of last season, and so far reports are favourable. The premises have been given a thorough facelift, making it a welcome place to get a take-away or enjoy a tasty burger (from €4), hot dog (€3), vegi burger (€3.50) or burrito (€4). If you're a real burger fan then pick up a pass – once you've had 10, the next one is free.

Dolce Vita

T: 05446 30279

Dorfstrasse 61, past the Spar (in the direction of Nasserein) on the left-hand side of the road, near Maximilian's restaurant, 12pm-midnight.

Don't let the modern building put you off from eating at this Italian-run pizzeria. The entrance hall may feel like you're in an urban car park, but cruise up the stairs and you'll find a smart, open-plan restaurant with arguably the best (and certainly longest!) pasta and risotto menu in St Anton. An extensive wine list compliments the freshly-made Italian and meat dishes. There's plenty of space so this is a good choice for large groups. Conveniently, Taxi Harry has a small office below to take you safely home.

Dorf Stub'n

T: 05446 2714

Dorfstrasse 60, towards the eastern end of the pedestrian zone, in between Hazienda and Bobo's restaurants, 6-11pm.

Traditional Tyrolean restaurant which loves its meat! Spacious enough to accommodate groups, you'll have a relaxed time and find a menu that doesn't give you any surprises, only well-cooked authentic food. Main course prices range from €17.50-24. House wine is reasonably priced (€11.90).

Floriani
T: 05446 2330

Alte Arlbergstrasse 13, from the roundabout at the western end of the village walk up the road that takes you past Sport Huber on your left; the restaurant is 100m further on, 5-10.45pm (closed Mondays), no reservations.

A cosy restaurant, less hectic and noisy than Pizza Pomodoro (page 97). One of the original pizzerias in the village, it is well-known and reliable. An impressive 22 types of pizza, including good vegetarian options such as goat's cheese and rocket. Pasta (€7.20-€10.60), ribs (€9.80) and classic Austrian cuisine (€9.90-14.40) are also available.

Le Fonti
T: 05446 42650

Dorfstrasse 14, on the right-hand side of the pedestrian zone, 50m from the tourist office, 6pm till late.

Le Fonti is run by the same owners as the Bifangalm restaurant on

Rendl (page 120), and offers the same reliable range of good quality Tyrolean dishes made from local produce, including roast venison, beef and lamb (€13.90-19.90). The authentic, rustic interior is one of the best in the traditional range in St Anton making it a definite Mad Dog favourite.. Friendly staff, a cosy atmosphere and an enjoyable experience – not forgetting the superb wine list, which is surprisingly lengthy.

Fuhrmann Stube
T: 05446 2921

Dorfstrasse 74, 50m down from the Spar supermarket, walking in the direction of Nasserein,

opposite Maximilian's restaurant, 4-11.30pm.

This traditional Tyrolean stube is one of St Anton's long-established restaurants and is popular with locals and returning guests alike. All that you'd expect from an authentic kitchen, including a good choice of knödels (€8.50-11.50), toasts (€4.20-5.60) and schnitzel (€10.60). Smoky but cosy, warm and inviting; it's a good place to be when the snow is falling outside.

Grieswirt

T: 05446 2965

Im Gries 4, next to Pub 37 on the road to the Post Office (turn right

off Dorfstrasse just before Parfumerie Bano), 6.30-10pm.

Housed in one of the older buildings of St Anton, this restaurant offers a true Tyrolean experience. A lot of German guests come here, so expect a vibrant atmosphere and lots of beery cheer. Because it's not on the main drag, it often gets passed by. All the usual favourites are on the menu; schnitzel (€14.90), spaghetti (€7.90) and steak (€19.30).

Häferl

T: 05446 3988

Dorfstrasse 18, near the tourist office (opposite Intersport), from 7.30am.

Inviting (and a little smoky) this tea room is conveniently located in the centre of the village. Settle into the steamy warmth for tea and Austrian cake at the end of the day or sit around the bar in the alcove areas to enjoy a glühwein. There are also snacks, including quite a few meaty ones; Tyrolean sausages or Bavarian white sausages (both around €5). Breakfast served between 7.30 and 10am.

Hax'n Stub'n

T: 05446 3870

Kandaharweg 2, at the roundabout near the taxi rank (western end of the resort), near Galzigbahn and

Gampen chair, 10am-8pm, (reservations after 7pm only).

Local family-run restaurant with a strong authentic kitchen and relaxed atmosphere. The cooking is good, the food is filling and the menu offers lots of opportunities to sample traditional dishes; spätzle (€8.95-12.80), wurstle (€9.60) and one of the few places in resort to serve schweinhaxe (pig's trotters) (€10.70). The 'WM platter' (wings, steak and ribs for €25.10) is a popular dish to share between two. The restaurant's proximity to the piste means it can get particularly busy between 1-2pm. Don't sit too close to the kitchen unless you like the strong smell of schnitzel cooking!

Hazienda

T: 05446 2968

Dorfstrasse 56, towards the eastern end of the pedestrian zone, 6.30-10pm, (reservations recommended).

The Hazienda has maintained its upmarket wine-bar chic for over 20 years in St Anton and is still a firm favourite, particularly with the 30-something age group. With a relaxed, laid-back atmosphere it's perfect for entertaining friends, enjoying celebrations or a romantic evening. Staff are friendly, efficient and seem to genuinely enjoy their job. The menu is international and Italian; homemade pasta (€13-15),

Argentinean beef (€24) and Indonesian noodles (€13.50). Add to this the good wine (house wine €27) and cocktail list and the place is a guaranteed hit. Starting in the 2006/7 season, the restaurant shares an entrance with the new Testa Rossa café.

Hospiz Alm

T: 05446 3625
W: www.hospizalm.at

lunchtime   **evening**

In the centre of St Christoph (just before the St Christoph 4-man chairlift, at the bottom of 8 (St Christoph)), 9.30am-12pm (supper from 7pm), evening reservations necessary.

Out of town but definitely worth the trip for a special occasion. Original, rustic, stylish; the Hospiz Alm serves authentic Tyrolean food with warm and careful hospitality. Within the restaurant there are private rooms, big tables for groups to share, tucked-away tables for two and – surprisingly – a slide that takes you down to the loos in the basement (actually for transporting cases of wine to the extensive cellar!). The whole roasted duck, served in two courses (€49 for two people) is delicious and beautifully presented. Other evening options include saddle of deer with creamed brussel-sprout leaves and chestnut brioche (€27.60) and roast pheasant (€28.40). Wednesday is fondue evening.

A taxi from St Anton costs around €30 one-way in the evening.

The restaurant is also open for lunch (outside on the terrace is best) with a simpler, cheaper menu. Try the enormous plate of spare ribs (€14.80) or the cheese spätzle (€12.20). Ice-bar après-ski from 4pm.

Kandahar

T: 05446 30260

Dorfstrasse 50, centre of the pedestrian zone, opposite the fountain, 7pm-6am (food served until 11pm), (reservations taken for both supper and drink-only tables).

Before the dancing starts, curry is served in this popular night club. See page 110.

Maximilian

Dorfstrasse 57, past the Spar (in the direction of Nasserein) on the left-hand side of the road, 11am-11pm.

One of the newer restaurants in town, Maximilian's has built up a healthy business based on its well-priced home cooking and friendly, efficient staff. With a mixture of comfortable (schnitzel, baked potatoes and steaks) to not-so-comfortable (calf's head) food, this is a popular choice for families as it's child-friendly and located near

many of the hotels at this end of the resort.

Montjola

T: 05446 2302

Gastigweg 29, from the roundabout at the western end of the village walk up the road (Alte Arlbergstrasse) that takes you past Hotel Schindler. Gastigweg is the steep road that exits to the right – keep plodding uphill until you see the restaurant on your right.
The walk from the centre takes about 10-15 minutes; alternatively hop in a taxi. Open from 6.30pm.

Whilst riding high on its reputation as the best fondue restaurant in St

Anton, Montjola still takes a lot of care and is worth a visit, particularly if you are staying nearby. The traditional but simple décor is unpretentious and has a pleasant faded feel. Starters are available (€4.70-11) but why bother when you can go straight to the fantastic fondue (€23-28.50) and then finish with a chocolate version (€18). Other classic Austrian dishes such as wiener schnitzel (€17) are also available. The restaurant is popular with groups visiting on their chalet-staff night off - if you'd rather avoid the crowds make a reservation on a night other than Wednesday or Thursday.

Museum restaurant

T: 05446 2475

Rudi-Matt-Weg 10, from the roundabout at the western end of the village walk up Alte Arlbergstrasse and follow signs to the Museum up a winding path off to the right, 6-10pm (closed Mondays), reservations essential.

One of the most beautiful buildings in St Anton, the Museum was originally built in 1912 as a mansion for a German industrialist but is now owned by the local community. The main part of the building holds this superb formal restaurant, complete with a huge open fireplace and

authentic Tyrolean interior. There are also private rooms available for groups. Locally sourced produce is used to create a variety of dishes, including roast beef, wild venison, trout and duck (€15-25). A warm atmosphere, created by their young team and accomplished chef.

Pizza Pomodoro

T: 05446 3333

Dorfstrasse 5, at the western end of the pedestrian zone next to Platzl bar, 6-10.30pm, (no reservations or take-aways).

With its bubbly atmosphere and friendly staff, Pizza Pomodoro offers the best and cheapest pizza in St Anton and as a result it's packed, particularly from around 7.30pm. Set like a traditional pizzeria, it has everything you'd expect from a great Italian kitchen where pizza dough and pasta are made on the premises. Daily specials and a delicious homemade lasagne are added to the menu of pizzas (€6.80-8.90) and pastas (around €8).

Restaurant Post Stuben
T: 05446 22130

In the Hotel Post on Dorfstrasse; in the centre of the resort opposite the Sport Hotel, 11.30am-2pm, 6.30-9.30pm.

One of the more upmarket restaurants is housed in this central 4-star hotel. Separate from the hotel's restaurant for its guests, the Post Stuben is set in a traditional interior with little corner tables and benches in the Austrian style. The haute cuisine Tyrolean menu includes calf saddle (€14), trout (€24), warm salads (€12-16) and excellent steak (€28). The food is matched with a quiet ambiance and attentive service.

Rodelalm
T: 0699 1085 8855

Above the village; take Nassereinbahn to Gampen.

From there, follow the signs to Rodelbahn. The alm is about half-way down the track on the right-hand side, reservations essential.

This is a truly great Austrian experience for young, old, first-timers and the worldly-wise! Toboggan (or ski) in the day to enjoy the alm as a mountain restaurant or, better still, hire a rodel on a Tuesday or Thursday evening (see page 140), toboggan part way down and stop off, rosy-cheeked, for supper. Complete with a cosy central fire, the atmosphere is welcoming and the hearty food is excellent - including the infamous pig's trotters (€15.50) and one of the largest schnitzels in St Anton. Gröstl (€10.50) and ribs (€16) are also good. Definitely not first choice for vegetarians!

Romantic Burg
T: 05446 31440

Nassereinerstrasse 49, half-way up the street; opposite San Antonio pizzeria, 4-11.30pm.

With both a fancy-looking dining area and an authentic Tyrolean stube, the owners take great pride in their hospitality and food. A quieter restaurant than most with a menu that includes interesting dishes such as duck breast (€21.50), pike (€16.80) and roast lamb (€23.50). Although not a vegetarian restaurant, there are options such as vegetable tart and tagliatelle. Unusually for St Anton, there is a cover charge (€3.80), but don't let this put you off as the food is worth it.

Café-Restaurant Sailer
T: 05446 2673

Dorfstrasse 4, at the far west end of the village, opposite the roundabout, 11am-10pm.

More of a large café than a restaurant, Sailer is a well-established haunt for returning guests (mostly Germanic) and their ski-instructors. Dated in its drab interior, made browner by age-old smoke, it isn't the most enticing environment. However if you're on a budget the prices may lure you in; pizza (€8.50), soups (€3.40-5) and wurstl (€3-7).

San Antonio Pizzeria
T: 05446 3474

Nassereinerstrasse 38, halfway up the street, opposite Romantic Burg, 6-11pm.

One of the best restaurants in Nasserein, located within the 4-star Aparthotel San Antonio. Local dishes join an extensive Italian menu, including a range of pasta (€4.20-10.80). The pizzas (€6.90-10.70) are prepared in a traditional oven in the open kitchen. The

restaurant is busy with guests who are staying both in Nasserein and the centre of St Anton. Take-aways available.

Restaurant Schindler
T: 05446 2207

Alte Arlbergstrasse 16, from the western end of the village walk up the road that takes you past Sport Huber on your left; 80m on the right you find the restaurant, 6-10.30pm.

Located in the grand-looking 3-star Hotel Schindler, this is a quiet restaurant, frequented by hotel guests but also popular with locals. Traditional décor accompanies a mix of regional and European dishes; for example gröstl (€11.90) and veal with truffle polenta (€17.50). Slightly formal atmosphere, which may hush momentarily when you walk in, but a good choice if you feel like a quieter evening amongst German-speakers.

Scotty's
T: 05446 2400

Gemeindegasse; turn right off the pedestrian zone on Dorfstrasse just before the Sport Hotel; it's near the pharmacy, 11am-10pm.

Scotty's is the bar/restaurant of Hotel Rosanna, one of Mark Warner's hotels in the resort.

Unsurprisingly it is a popular hang-out for the resort's UK reps and chalet staff – and their guests. Mainly serving pizzas (around €12) the quality of food and service varies considerably from year to year. Other dishes include fajitas (€13.50), nachos (€4.90) and lasagne (€8.50). Perhaps not the finest dining in town, but with dance music and litres of enticing green cocktails, it's a fun place for Brits looking for a big night out.

Steakhouse
T: 05446 3111

In the Sport Hotel on Dorfstrasse; slap in the centre of the resort, opposite Hotel Post, 11am-11pm.

Another good hotel restaurant. Despite the American overtones of a 'steakhouse', this restaurant is distinctly European with a strong Austrian flavour. Local steak (€22.90-33.60) plus soups, salads and snacks. There is also a good wine list, and a champagne and cocktail bar for a welcome aperitif.

S'Wirtshaus am Alten Bahnhof
T: 05446 30145

Walter-Schuler-Weg 5, near the small man-made lake on the track opposite the Well.com centre, 6-10pm.

Located in the old train station, although not many reminders of its

working past exist apart from the building itself, the S'Wirtshaus is popular with locals, including the former railway workers. Having said that, visitors to the resort who dine there are more than welcome. Fried fish, schnitzel and goulash (all €11.50) are just some of the dishes on the simple menu (main course prices range from €5.10-11.50). Can be a little smoky and greasy, but the place has character and a jovial atmosphere. Get there early to find a table as it fills up quickly.

Testa Rossa

Dorfstrasse, towards the eastern end of the pedestrian zone (shares an entrance with Hazienda restaurant and can also be accessed from Nah & Frisch

*supermarket), 8am-1am
(lunch:12-2pm, supper: 6-10pm),
no reservations.*

New for the 2006/7 season, this
round-the-clock (or near enough)
café will remind you more of where
you buy your coffee on the way to
work than a traditional Alpine
coffee bar. It looks promising,
though; for breakfast you can have
coffee, pastries and marmalade
(€6), for lunch there's a wide
selection of paninis (from €4.20)
and salads (€10-11) and the day
winds up with an Italian-based
supper menu (including various
pastas). In between choose from
numerous coffees, beers and
wines. If you're waiting for a table
at Hazienda, have a drink here to
pass the time.

Tom Dooley's
T: 05446 3388

 LATE

*Nassereinerstrasse 21, five
minutes' walk up from
Nassereinbahn (heading away from
the village), set back off the road
on the left-hand side, 3pm-1/2am
(food service stops around 11pm).*

Nasserein's popular local pub.
See page 113.

Underground on the Piste
T: 05446 2000

*Rudi-Matt-Weg 9, from the
roundabout at the western end of
the village walk up Alte Arlberg-*

*strasse and follow signs to the
Museum; you will see the restaurant
on your left, near the piste, lunch:
from 11am, supper: 6-10.30pm.*

A well-known establishment to
those skiers who return to St Anton
year after year. Set in a Tyrolean
wooden house, the cosy
atmosphere is complimented by
live music, board games and plenty
of flowing Irish beer. It's a place to
have a good chat, feel laidback and
eat a delicious variety of food
including grills, seafood, fondues
and wok dishes (price range €5-
20). You'll often find live acoustic
music in the afternoon – a more
serene après-ski than the Moose or
KK (page 124). It's a 30-second
ski, or a two minute walk, back to
the village from here.

Après-ski and nightlife

Après-ski in St Anton starts early! It isn't unusual to see people settled into a bar by 3 or 4pm, particularly at those places that start to pump out loud music around that time.

Most people who have been to St Anton will mention the Krazy Kanguruh, Taps and Mooserwirt (see pages 111 and 112) as the major slope-side players, and it's true that the energy and volume they exude makes them impressive.

For a more laidback end to your day, there are other mountain restaurants offering a more peaceful haven, where you can enjoy the view and wind down over a few mugs of glühwein.

Après-ski in the village offers various options. There are fewer dedicated bars than you might expect; many places are combined restaurant/bars, although this

How read our reviews:

– budget: small beer cost around €3

– mid-range: small beer costs €3-5

– expensive: small beer costs over €5

`LATE` – venues that close late (1am or after)

– our absolute **Mad Dog** favourites (page 87)

needn't hamper your enjoyment. You can cram into the Anton bar for a Red Bull Boot (page 107), cosy up in the Underground (page 113), hang out in the tiny Pub 37 (page 112), relax over tea and cakes at the Häferl café (page 93) or enjoy a beer and tapas at Bodega (page 108).

As with the restaurants, most bars are located in the pedestrian zone of Dorfstrasse; easy to find, and easy to move on to the next venue. Be aware that some restaurants and bars either forbid ski boots completely (on the basis that they 'damage the floors') or do so after 8pm.

For late-night bars, try to get there before 10.30pm to avoid the queues that build up. If you're looking to stay out till dawn, then Platzl and Bar Cuba (pages 111 and 108) stay open until 3am, with Kandahar and Postkeller closing at 6am during peak season (pages 110 and 111). Challenge yourself to a full twelve hours of après-ski in St Anton!

Our favourite bars

Anton – page 107.	Slick après-ski bar with fresh DJs every couple of weeks
Bobo's – page 107.	Friendly basement bar with live music and karaoke nights
Fang House – page 109	Nasserein's buzzing après-ski venue
Funky Chicken – page 109.	Classic St Anton nightlife in the heart of the village
Platzl – page 111.	Drinks by candlelight followed by dancing
Underground on the Piste – page 113.	Relaxed drinking beside the piste

Live music

Many bars have informal live music occasionally. You'll find more regular entertainment in the following venues. This was last season's schedule, so check with bar staff to see what's changed:

Bobo's – page 107.

A variety of live music is enthusiastically played in this friendly basement bar on Tuesdays, Wednesdays and Sundays. Arrive early to secure a table or seat at the bar. If you're hungry, good Mexican food is served

Bodega – page 108.

Rosella plays her guitar and sings every Wednesday and Thursday. Enjoy some tapas and a beer while you listen

Bar Cuba – page 108.

There's live music here most nights in February and March, between 8-11pm. Normally acoustic covers

Underground on the Piste – page 113.

Various live music nights take place in this cosy piste-side bar/restaurant. Ask for details

Alibi

T: 05446 3172

Dorfstrasse 78, down from Spar supermarket (in the direction of the church), opposite Dolce Vita pizzeria, 4pm-1am.

Everything you'd expect from a traditional pub – locals, smoking, beer, dark wood and bric-a-brac. Tyrolean background music.

Anton bar

T: 05446 2408
W: www.anton-aparthotel.com

Kandaharweg 4, right opposite Galzigbahn, 11am-9pm.

Part of the Aparthotel Anton complex, offering a variation on the usual table-dancing après-ski. DJ from 4-9pm (a new one flies into resort every two weeks). The bar fills up very quickly between 3-9pm and in bad weather it's busy all day. Popular with the English and frequented by local ski instructors after their day on the hill, come along to unwind and get into a party mood. Until 8.45pm you can order food from the same menu as the Anton restaurant next door (page 87). There's a good range of beers as well as excellent cocktails (€7.20-9.90 - their Caipirinha is worth trying) and beers. Red Bull Boot (bottle of vodka plus five Red Bulls) is a popular option (€95).

Ben.Venuto

T: 05446 30203
W: www.benvenuto.at

Hannes-Schneider-Weg 1; on the first-floor of the Well.com centre (opposite the old railway station), 6.30pm-midnight.

At quieter times (for example in the early evening) you can have a drink at the long bar in this upmarket restaurant. Good wine list. See page 88.

Bobo's

T: 05446 271454
W: www.bobos.at

Dorfstrasse 60, towards the eastern end of the pedestrian zone, next to Dorf Stub'n restaurant, 6-11pm (bar open till 1am).

Lively basement restaurant with a popular bar and live music. See page 89.

Bodega

T: 05446 42788

Dorfstrasse, across the street from Hotel Post, 3pm-1am.

Friendly tapas bar in the resort centre. See page 90.

Bar Cuba

T: 0664 6523886

Dorfstrasse 33, at the eastern end of the pedestrian zone, opposite Aquila restaurant, 8pm-3am (also open 12-4pm at weekends for major sporting events).

Definitely a Brit hang-out, with Sky Sports shown on the central screen and in every corner. Not the swishest bar but with friendly, fun staff and people out to have a good time, Bar Cuba will remind you of your local. There are even Pukka Pies to fill the gap if you get homesick. Tuesdays and Wednesdays are jam packed. Live music (8-11pm) most nights in February and March (generally acoustic covers). There's occasional dancing, but it's more of a bar than a club.

Fang House
T: 0676 4091010

Nassereinerstrasse 6, at the base of 24 (Stallmähder-Fang), on skier's right of Nassereinbahn, 10am-10pm.

Convenient if you are skiing back to Nasserein, the Fang House is a busy, vibrant bar – the best one at this end of St Anton. Inside gets packed as weary skiers retire for the day. Parents can relax on the terrace and watch their kids practising on the nearby slopes. Order at the bar (with a struggle) or wait for table service. Hot chocolate and rum (€4.50) and glühwein (€3.80) are both good. Strongbow cider and Guinness are also available. There's only one loo for women so plan ahead!

Funky Chicken
T: 05446 30201

Dorfstrasse 7, western end; set back behind Pizza Pomodoro, 6pm-2am.

No visit to St Anton would be complete without a night at the infamous and seriously popular Funky Chicken. Renowned for the best party atmosphere in town, courtesy of the Funky crew, you're guaranteed a great time thanks to the blend of freshly-made food (chicken and chips €8, curries €6-9), reasonably-priced drinks (margaritas €4-5.50, beer €2.80) and a different DJ every night. Come along early enough and you can lounge in the cushioned area and watch the latest ski videos. Arrive before 10.30pm or risk the long, cold queue.

Hazienda
T: 05446 2968

Dorfstrasse 56, towards the eastern end of the pedestrian zone, shares an entrance with Testa Rossa café, 6.30-10pm.

Primarily a restaurant, you can enjoy an early evening drink in this wine bar before the crowds arrive. See page 94.

Kandahar

T: 05446 30260

Dorfstrasse 50, centre of the pedestrian zone, opposite the fountain, 7pm-6am (food served until 11pm), (reservations taken for both supper and drink-only tables).

The main nightclub for UK holiday-makers in St Anton is named after Lord Kandahar, a British general who established the Arlberg-Kandahar Race with Hannes Schneider. Reflecting its Eastern-style décor, earlier on in the evening Kandahar serves delicious Thai and Indian food (green chicken curry and chicken vindaloo are both €13) until swinging into club mode from 10pm. Guest DJs, including big Ibiza names, continue to fill the dance-floor until 6am. It's normally pretty quiet until about midnight but try to arrive before 1am or hit queues and a €5 cover charge. Beers start at €3.50, long drinks are around €8.

Krazy Kanguruh

T: 05446 2633

Lifts: on the home-run,
1 (Zammermoos-St Anton),
Pedestrian: catch the bus (Line 3)
up to the Mooserkreuz stop, follow
the road towards the piste (it is
well-signed); the bar is across the
piste at the back of Taps.

Loud, legendary St Anton après-ski starts here. See mountain restaurants page 124.

Mooserwirt

T: 05446 3588

Lifts: on the home-run,
1 (Zammermoos-St Anton),

Pedestrian: catch the bus (Line 3)
up to the Mooserkreuz stop, follow
the road towards the piste (it is
well-signed).

Piste-side dancing in your ski boots. See mountain restaurants page 124.

Platzl

T: 05446 2169

Dorfstrasse 3, western end; next
to Pizza Pomodoro, 7pm-3am.

Rustic and homely, you're wise to get to Platzl early to claim one of the comfy sofas upstairs and relax in the intimate atmosphere over a candle-lit drink. Offering the same menu as Pizza Pomodoro (page

97) from 7-10pm, things get increasingly lively after that. The downstairs bar area has a dance-floor for enjoying an eclectic mix of jazz, rock, pop and house. Drinks are reasonably priced with beers at €3, and long drinks/cocktails between €7-12. No ski boots after 8pm. The cloakroom charge is €2 well-spent, as it keeps your coat out of the smoky bar. Platzl will be under new management in the 2006/7 season; hopefully any changes will only enhance this old favourite.

Postkeller

T: 05446 22130

Dorfstrasse 13, under the Hotel

Post (entrance door leads to both Piccadilly après-ski bar and Postkeller nightclub) 9.30pm-6am.

The largest and longest-running nightclub in St Anton, Postkeller is the haunt of (mainly) German and Dutch holiday-makers. A slightly older crowd, the place has a constant flow of people coming from the Piccadilly bar, and post-dinner crowds looking to continue the night. Mainstream pop/dance music is played. There are a lot of guys and women get in free – a good idea to encourage female tourists; it helps dilute the drunk mass of beefcakes in this well-known cattle market! Entrance fee for men €5, cocktails €5-10, glass of wine €4.80.

Pub 37
T: 05446 2965

Im Gries 4, turn right off Dorfstrasse (heading down towards Nasserein) just before Parfumerie Bano, 5pm-2am.

The smallest bar in resort – 20 people inside and it's full. Run by a local, Heidi, the atmosphere is cosy and smoky and drinking beer seems obligatory (from €3 for a small glass). Mostly frequented by a regular crowd; if you fancy meeting some of the locals and practising your German, this is a friendly place to start. No ski boots after 8pm.

Scotty's
T: 05446 2400

Gemeindegasse; turn right off the pedestrian zone in Dorfstrasse, just before the Sport Hotel; it's near the pharmacy, 11am-10pm.

The restaurant/bar attached to Mark Warner's hotel. Particularly popular with young Brits. See page 101.

Taps
T: 05446 2628

Lifts: on the home-run,
1 (Zammermoos-St Anton),
Pedestrian: catch the bus (Line 3)

up to the Mooserkreuz stop, follow the road towards the piste (it is well-signed); the bar is across the piste.

Enjoy budget drinks, shots and snacks at this popular après-ski bar. See mountain restaurants page 126.

Testa Rossa

Dorfstrasse, towards the eastern end of the pedestrian zone (shares an entrance with Hazienda restaurant), 8am-1am (lunch:12-2pm, supper: 6-10pm), no reservations.

Modern café and bar, new for the 2006/7 season. See page 102.

Tom Dooley's
T: 05446 3388

Nassereinerstrasse 21, located about five minutes' walk up the road from Nassereinbahn (walking away from the village), tucked away on the left-hand side, 3pm-1/2am (food service stops around 11pm).

Popular with all sorts; locals playing cards in the afternoon and English and Scandinavian visitors in the evening. Tom Dooley's is run by a charismatic local who, apart from holding the prestigious title of President of the Kandahar Ski Club, plays a mean blues and jazz clarinet when the mood takes him. More of a pub than a bar, serving Guinness alongside Austrian beers. Bar snacks only – pizzas (€6.20-7), soups (from €2.90), frankfurters and burgers (€2.60-4.50).

Underground on the Piste
T: 05446 2000

Rudi-Matt-Weg 9, from the roundabout at the western end of the village walk up Alte Arlbergstrasse and follow signs to the Museum; you will see the building on your left, near the piste, lunch from 11am, supper 6-10.30pm.

Laidback, piste-side restaurant/bar housed in a traditional chalet. See page 103.

Vino bar

T: 05446 22440

Dorfstrasse 35, at the eastern end of the pedestrian zone, next to the Schwarzer Adler hotel, 8pm-2am plus.

The only real 'lounge' bar in St Anton, Vino is a cool place to relax in comfy armchairs with a good cocktail (around €8) or glass of wine. The décor is a bit 90s, with a casino/wine-bar feel but it's a nice change from the hectic bars further along the pedestrian zone. There are occasional football screenings.

Mountain restaurants

Because you don't always know where you'll end up on the mountain, we review each and every restaurant shown on the official piste map, whether good, bad or indifferent. Mountain restaurants are listed alphabetically and by resort or area (ie St Anton/ St Christoph/Rendl, Stuben and Sonnenkopf, Zürs/Lech/Oberlech).

The food choice on the mountain tends to be more uniform than in resort; the focus is generally on local dishes, perhaps supplemented with some pasta or pizza. Prices are a little higher than in the resort, especially over in Lech and Oberlech. Make sure you take some cash with you, as not everywhere accepts credit cards.

Most restaurants open and close with the lifts, although food service is likely to finish after lunch time (a little later in self-service places).

To interpret our symbols see page 87.

Finding your restaurant:

In this section you'll find reviews for all of the restaurants marked on the official piste map. Rather unhelpfully, these restaurants appear on the map as a knife and fork symbol, rather than by name. Mad Dog have created our own maps (page 116) and numbered each restaurant review. The number corresponds to our maps.Because our books are pocket-sized, you'll probably still need to cross-refer to your piste map to navigate your way to the restaurant you have chosen.

St Anton also has some great places to have lunch that are not shown on the piste map but are very close to the piste. We have reviewed these as well and they're shown on our mountain restaurant map numbered in blue, rather than red. Don't forget that lots of restaurants in the village also open for lunch.

Where possible we set out the best way for pedestrians to reach mountain restaurants. However, quite a few of the more remote ones are inaccessible unless you are on skis.

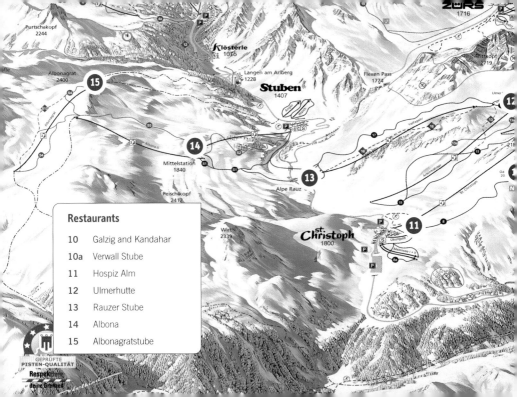

Restaurants

10	Galzig and Kandahar
10a	Verwall Stube
11	Hospiz Alm
12	Ulmerhutte
13	Rauzer Stube
14	Albona
15	Albonagratstube

Restaurants

1 Rendl Beach
2 Bifangalm
3 Mooserwirt
4 Taps
5 Krazy Kanguruh
6 Fang House
7 Gampen
8 Kapall
9 Valluga

Restaurants

16	Bundehutte
17	Berg Restaurant Sonnenkopf
18	Berg Restaurant Seekopf
19	Schrofli Alm
20	Berghaus Tritt-Alpe
21	Panorama
22	Rud-Alpe
22a	Hotel Goldener Berg
23	Kriegeralpe
24	Palmenalpe

Our favourite mountain restaurants

Albona, Stuben – page 127.	Enjoy a budget Austrian lunch in this pretty resort
Hotel Goldener Berg, Oberlech – page 130.	Not cheap, but you can choose from an imaginative menu on the hotel's fantastic sunny terrace
Hospiz Alm, St Christoph – page 123.	Unmissable traditional restaurant in the village of St Christoph
Palmenalpe, Lech – page 131.	Perched over the piste, relax in a deckchair at this popular outside bar
Rendl Beach, Rendl – page 125.	Good value, sunny restaurant and bar at the top of the Rendl gondola
Schröfli Alm, Zürs – page 134.	Above-average prices but welcoming and full of character with a large terrace and ice-bar overlooking the Alpine peaks
Ulmerhütte, St Anton - page 126	A popular mountain hut for over 100 years

Bifangalm (2)
(St Anton: Rendl)
T: 05446 30238
    0664 2302220

Lifts: from Rendl Beach, ski
R1 (Rendl Talabfahrt) down to
the village. Located on your right,
on last 200m of the run,
Pedestrian: no daytime access,
evening access (Thursdays and
Fridays) via piste-basher,
(reservations for evenings only).

Dark, cosy and smoky, with a small
terrace (you may need to avoid the
tables nearest to the enthusiastic
Tyrolean music!) this traditional
restaurant (which isn't marked on
your piste map) gets busy on sunny

days. A good place to drop in for a
last hot chocolate with apple strudel
or schnapps on your way home.
There's a straightforward menu of
local dishes; frankfurters (€4.50),
pastas (€7.80-9.10) and good
speckbrot (€9.40). A surprisingly
large wine cellar with over 150
international and Austrian wines.
Thursday and Friday nights are
busy for the fondue/BBQ evenings
(some UK tour operators
recommend this to their clients).

Fang House (6)
(St Anton)
T: 0676 4091010

Nassereinerstrasse 6, at the base
of 24 (Stallmähder-Fang), on skier's

right of Nassereinbahn, Lifts/
Pedestrian: at the base of
Nassereinbahn, 10am-10pm.

More of a bar than a mountain
restaurant, this is the ideal place
for a final glühwein if you're staying
in Nasserein. See page 109.

Galzig and Kandahar (10)
(St Anton)
T: 05446 2352501

Lifts/Pedestrian: at the top of
Galzigbahn.

This busy junction - from where
skiers head to the pistes of
Osthang, St Christoph or up to
Valluga - is served by three
restaurants (see also the more

upmarket Verwall Stube page 127). Two of them, Galzig and Kandahar (the latter is upstairs), are self-service and have the same menu. They may not have the most refined atmosphere, with their sparse wooden tables and benches, but the views through the large windows are impressive enough to distract you and there's plenty of space to sit. Canteen options include a dish of the day (eg schnitzel €10.40), pizza (€3.80 a slice), a good salad bar (€4.90) and roast chicken (€8.90).

Gampen (7)
(St Anton)
T: 05446 2352532

Lifts: Gampen 4-man chairlift, Pedestrian: take Nassereinbahn and walk 50m down the piste.

As one of the most central restaurants on the mountain, it does get very busy here. You'll find a large terrace at the back along with an ice-bar. Average self-service food such as lasagne (€8.30) and frankfurters (€3.90), and the dish of the day is usually good value (for example baked fish and salad €8.40). Wine is surprisingly expensive (around €23-28). Open on Tuesday and Thursday evenings until 10pm (with live, cheesy music) for those tobogganing – however the nearby Rodelalm (page 98) offers a more rustic experience.

Hospiz Alm (11)
(St Christoph)

T: 05446 3625
W: www.hospizalm.at

evening   **lunchtime**

Lifts: ski down 8 (St Christoph) from the top of Galzig, the restaurant is on the right near base, just before the St Christoph chairlift, Pedestrian: two minutes' walk from the centre of St Christoph (you can catch the Post Bus or a taxi there from St Anton); on the opposite side of the road to the Hospiz hotel, towards the piste.

Rustic and very popular restaurant in the beautiful village of St Christoph. See page 94.

Kapall (8)
(St Anton)

T: 05446 2352532

Lifts: 100m down from the top of Kapall 6-man chairlift, on the left, Pedestrian: no access.

Small, self-service restaurant with a sun-terrace which can get covered in cloud, hiding the otherwise magnificent view across the peaks. A very meaty menu, with classic dishes such as speckbrot (€4.80), schnitzel (€10.90) and goulash (€6.10/9.10). The service area downstairs is small, which means the queue tends to be long and slow, but a small bar allows you to get drinks much quicker.

Seating areas are available upstairs and down.

Krazy Kanguruh (5)
(St Anton)
T: 05446 2633

Lifts: on the home-run, 1 (Zammermoos-St Anton), Pedestrian: catch the bus (Line 3) up to the Mooserkreuz stop, follow the road towards the piste (it is well-signed); the bar is across the piste at the back of Taps, (reservations taken).

St Anton's original après-ski venue, the KK is vibrant and full on. Burger and chips (€9.50) combine with fajitas (€6.90) and frankfurters (€8)

to make an international budget menu. But with three bars for you to enjoy, food isn't really the point! Thursday nights are particularly popular with UK guests, when the party atmosphere is set alight by 'shot girls' squirting liquor from their guns, cocktails like the KK killer and, just to add more humour, an indoor snow-machine. Arrive before the busiest time of 4-5pm. Ski check €2.

Mooserwirt (3)
(St Anton)
T: 05446 3588

Lifts: on the home-run, 1 (Zammermoos-St Anton),

Pedestrian: catch the bus (Line 3) up to the Mooserkreuz stop, follow the road towards the piste (it is well-signed).

The Mooserwirt gives you an 'Oktoberfest' party every day. Set in a traditional building, the serving area extends outside to the famous round ice-bar, where skiers dancing on tables to euro-trash music is the norm. German beers (such as Weizenbier) are on tap, along with glühwein (€4.70). Standard dishes of burgers, ribs and pasta are priced between €12-16. Open until 8pm, be there before 3pm or it's impossible to get a seat amongst hundreds of tipsy, dancing skiers!

Rauzer Stube (13)
(Alpe Rauz)

Lifts/Pedestrian: located in the Alpe Rauz car park at the base of the Rauz T-bar (which takes you up to the Valfagehr 6-man chairlift), no telephone.

An Austrian version of a transport cafe; quite rare in these parts! Many of the people who work on the mountain treat this place as their local. Tourists tend to use the outside terrace for a quick beer in good weather. Food is available in the form of burgers (€3.50-4.50), vegi burger (€7), wurstl (€4-7) and spaghetti (€7) though it isn't the most inspiring place to stop for lunch. However, if you're hungry or waiting for a bus it'll do the job and prices are reasonable.

Rendl Beach (1)
(St Anton: Rendl)
T: 05446 2352550

Lifts/Pedestrian: at the top of Rendl gondola.

You'll see the outside bar as you exit the lift (near the giant snowman if there has been enough snow!) whilst the self-service restaurant and terrace are upstairs. The building is a bit 70s but there's a fantastically welcoming atmosphere. Although Rendl is often a quiet option, in good weather it can be packed as it gets the sun most of the day so queues do build up, especially between 12.30-2pm. Food includes good stir-fries (€10), huge helpings of pasta (€7.80) and a salad bar (from €4.90; great value if you stack!). Popular with novices for the nearby blue runs, it's also good for lazy people who want to spend the afternoon drinking, sunbathing, listening to music and watching beach volleyball. You can ski straight back to the resort from here at the end of the day.

Taps (4)
(St Anton)
T: 05446 2628

Lifts: on the home-run,
1 (Zammermoos-St Anton),

Pedestrian: catch the bus (Line 3) up to the Mooserkreuz stop, follow the road towards the piste (it is well-signed); the bar is across the piste.

Famous for its sun-terrace overlooking Rendl and St Anton, Taps is the perfect place to sit in a deckchair, soak up the sun, relax – or get into the party mood after a day's skiing. There's waiter service so you don't have to move a muscle to enjoy cheap drinks (beer, €3.80 for 0.5l; vodka-Red Bull shots €2) and snacks (burger and chips €9.50, ribs €10.60). With an ice-bar and two covered bar areas, Taps has a lively good-time feel whatever the weather. Happy hour (3-4pm) is the busiest time but the bar is open till 8pm.

Ulmerhütte (12)
(St Anton)
T: 0664 3075151

Lifts: take Arlenmähder 6-man chairlift, ski down 12 (Ulmerhütte) and it's on the left, Pedestrian: no access.

You really feel in the heart of the Arlberg at this mountain hut. At 103-years-old, it also receives house guests, most notably the German Alpine Club. Hearty Austrian favourites (schnitzel €11.90, fried cheese and potato €10.50) taste all the better for the incredible almost-360° views over the sweeping pistes. A warm refuge as you travel across the slopes on a big sky day.

Valluga (9)
(St Anton)
T: 05446 2352520

Lifts/Pedestrian: at the top of Valluga I cablecar.

With a panoramic view that enhances the otherwise plain and simple décor, at 2650m this is the highest restaurant in resort. Enjoy simple dishes such as soup (€3.60-4.30), toasts (€5.50-6.20) and schnitzel (€11.10) for surprisingly reasonable prices, considering the location. Afterwards take a trip up to Valluga (2811m) which has a wonderful view across the peaks. Remember that you're only allowed on the Valluga II gondola with your skis if you have an official guide with you (page 32). Somehow this whole experience has a James Bond 70s feel to it. Opening hours depend on weather conditions and can therefore be erratic; you should check information boards at base stations.

Verwall Stube (10a)
(St Anton)
T: 05446 2352501

Lifts/Pedestrian: at the top of Galzigbahn.

If you want to meet friends at a convenient location, but don't want a self-service (or budget!) meal, then this is a good option. Located through the Kandahar self-service restaurant (see above) the Verwall serves cordon bleu cuisine overlooking the mountain peaks. A sun-terrace with après-ski music and ice-bar allows you to enjoy the views. Choices include steak tartare (€21.50), carpaccio (€19.20) and a wider-than-usual selection of fish dishes (€23-28), including bouillabaisse.

Albona (14)
(Stuben)

Lifts: situated at the top of Albona I (2-man chairlift) which leaves from Stuben village, Pedestrian: no access, no telephone.

Albonagratstube (15)
(Stuben)

Lifts: take Albona II 2-man chairlift, ski down S4 (Sonnleiten), then take Albonagrat 2-man chairlift up to the peak, Pedestrian: no access, no telephone.

Set at Stuben mid-station, Albona is well-placed for sun and a cheaper-than-average (but still tasty) self-service mountain lunch. Toasted cheese sandwich (€4.20), spaghetti (€6.80) and wurstl (€3.30-6.40) are some of the options. The low prices mean that there is often a queue at lunchtime and finding a table inside may be hard, a problem that can be exacerbated by ski schools making block reservations. Outside however there is a large sun-terrace with picnic tables and a sweeping view over the mountains. A modern building by local standards but the historical information displayed inside about Hannes Schneider (page 16), who was born in the village, is interesting.

Small, classic hut set upon Albonagrat, with a terrace overlooking the Maroiköpfle. Not a place to hang out, but rather to wolf down a warming, budget meal from the self-service kitchen. A particular popular pit-stop for skiers who are heading off-piste. Wurstle (10 varieties!) ranges from €2.50-6.70, knödel €2.40-3.60 and goulash soup is €3.70.

Berg Restaurant Sonnenkopf (17)
(Sonnenkopf)

Lifts: near the top of the Sonnenkopf gondola, Pedestrian: 50m walk from the top of the Sonnenkopf gondola, no telephone.

American-feel self-service restaurant, centrally placed for the 'Schneeland' children's activities. Seating up to 400 people, it is one of the largest restaurants in the Arlberg and feels a bit overwhelming. Thankfully there are separate smoking and non-smoking areas. Deckchairs can be rented, so you can rest in the sun with a drink from the ice-bar while your kids take ski school! Not

surprisingly given the large number of children who eat here, the kids' menu is comprehensive and well-priced. Choices for adults include steak (€10.90) and frankfurters (€3.50-5.50).

Bündehutte (16)
(Sonnenkopf)

Lifts: take Sonnenkopf gondola up to the top, then ski down Sonnenkopf 1; on the right just above mid-station, Pedestrian: no access, no telephone.

A 400-year-old barn, with a little sun-terrace and oompah music. Easy to spot, it offers a convenient break for a snack lunch; chicken

curry (€6.90), wurstle (€3.50-6.90) and strudel (€3.80) are some of the most popular dishes. Run by two local ladies, they ensure you and the children have an enjoyable time, even if the food is quite simple.

Berghaus Tritt-Alpe (20)
(Zürs)
T: 0664 2831

*Lifts: take Trittalp 6-man chairlift, then 1 (**Hexenboden Standard**), joining 3 (**Familienabfahrt**); restaurant is on skier's right, Pedestrian: no access.*

A little difficult to get to (not recommended for novice skiers) this is the only ski-stop this side of

Zürs so take full advantage of its terrace, bar and hearty homemade food, such as schnitzel (€14.50) and gröstl (€13). Although prices are above average for self-service, the food is worth it. The restaurant is decorated with wooden skis and farming paraphernalia along with rustic furniture. Even when it's busy, staff are efficient so you shouldn't wait too long.

Berg Restaurant Seekopf (18) (Zürs)

T: 0664 2187

Lifts: at the top of the Seekopf or Zürsersee 4-man chairlift, Pedestrian: no access except by chairlift.

Like Stuben, Zürs can get windy and this is a handy self-service refuge, all the more welcome for the relaxed atmosphere created by the local owner. It's also ideal for easy days on the piste, and a convenient meeting place for groups. A mixture of European and Austrian meals are available; wurstle (€5.20), a good knödel soup (€4.60), spaghetti - with a choice of five different sauces (€8.50) - and chilli con carne (€9). Prices are at the lower end of mid-range. It's quite small inside, with standard décor, but cosy enough. The large terrace is a sun-trap so you can relax awhile after lunch on good weather days.

Hotel Goldener Berg (22A) (Oberlech)

T: 05583 22050
W: www.hospiz.com

Lifts: just above the Petersboden chairlift, near 34 (Kriegeralpe-Petersboden-Oberlech-Lech), Pedestrian: Bergbahn Oberlech cable car from Lech followed by a walk.

Although it's piste-side, you won't find the Goldener Berg marked on your piste map. Owned by the same company as the charming Hospiz Alm in St Christoph (page 94) the Goldener Berg is equally welcoming. The large sunny terrace has a buzzing bar where you can enjoy a drink while you wait for a table. The fenced off 'gourmet corner' - complete with sheep-skin chair covers - has a more elaborate menu and prices are firmly in the expensive bracket. On the standard menu however main course prices are slightly cheaper (around €12-20) and the food tends to be more imaginative than you find in many other mountain restaurants. Try the gravlax (€12.50), deer goulash with spätzle and red cabbage (€18.50) or tasty spinach dumplings with gorgonzola sauce (€12.80). Worth a visit, even if you usually avoid hotel restaurants. Main courses are only served until 2pm so arrive early.

Kriegeralpe (23)
(Lech)
T: 0664 4422697

Lifts: take up Kriegerhorn 6-man chairlift, then ski down 34 (Kriegeralpe-Petersboden-Oberlech-Lech); the restaurant is on skier's right, Pedestrian: no access.

Typical Tyrolean alm in the middle of the slope which is open all year round (it's also a hotel). A small but representative Austrian menu is served; roast pork and potatoes (€13.80), deer wurstl (€10.90), soup and dumplings (€5.90) and mixed cold platter (€13.80). The food prices are reasonable (for Lech) although the wine is quite

expensive (€26-38). Background music and a view of the piste-traffic entertain you while you eat.

Palmenalpe (24)
(Lech)
T: 05583 3312

Lifts: from the top of Kriegerhorn 6-man chairlift follow 34 (Kriegeralpe-Petersboden-Oberlech-Lech). Alternatively, reach it via the Zugerberg 2-man chairlift from Zug, Pedestrian: no access.

Like a crow's nest perched on a craggy cliff, the Palmenalpe's location helps it stand out from most of the other mountain restaurants in the region. The

restaurant is a traditional Tyrolean hut, staff wear local costume and serve straightforward food; salads (€8.50-11.50) and tasty pizzas (€9.10-12.30). A compact and very sunny terrace and champagne ice-bar overlook the stunning Zug Valley; order a drink and relax in a deckchair (be warned though that the music volume can sometimes make this difficult – especially when Queen is playing!). Get there early if you can to avoid the queues; if the bar is packed it may be quicker to go inside to get your drinks. To return to the piste, a ski-pulley system runs along the flat cat-track; grab the rope and be pulled along.

Panorama (21)
(Lech)
T: 0664 2525

Lifts/Pedestrian: at the top of Rüfikopf I.

This modern, recently-renovated restaurant doesn't really create much of an atmosphere but the terrace has a magnificent view across the Arlberg and is a fantastically scenic place to enjoy homemade food with background après-ski music. Both self-and table-service are available. A good variety of soups and salads along with bratwurst and sauerkraut (€9.50), mixed meat grill (€16.50) and pasta (€7-9). Vegetarian choices include spinach dumplings (€10). Wine prices are above-average (€24.50-44). A useful place for lunch on the less-busy side of the Lech ski slopes.

Rud-Alpe (22)
(Lech)
T: 0664 418250

Lifts: take 34 (Kriegeralpe-Petersboden-Oberlech-Lech) down from Schlegelkopf; the restaurant is on skier's right on the last stretch, below the small fun-park (marked with a 'kinder' symbol on the piste map), Pedestrian: no access.

The original and largest mountain restaurant in Lech, this is a popular venue for visitors, made desirable by its large sunny terrace overlooking the village and peaks. You'll find 'Lech-style' prices (ie higher than in other parts of the region) but good food and fun music will match your notion of what après-ski in Lech is about. Service slows down in busy periods. The range of wines (€26-42) will help while away your afternoon if you want to relax and enjoy the holiday mood. Evenings bring a calmer, more romantic feel, with dinner in the Altholz Rooms.

Schröfli Alm (19)
(Zürs)
T: 0664 3345

Lifts: from the top of Seekopf 4-man chairlift, ski down 17 (Seekopf Standard). The restaurant is near the base of the run near the lift station, Pedestrian: no access.

Another alm which is hundreds of years old, this is a historic mountain resting place in every way. Welcoming and full of character, it offers either a cheery inside restaurant or a large terrace and ice-bar overlooking the peaks. Prices are above average, with main courses ranging from €8.90-25. Choose from a variety of meat dishes and pastas. Worth visiting if you're in the area.

Can't ski? Won't ski? Too much snow or not enough...? Find out about **other things to do** in St Anton.

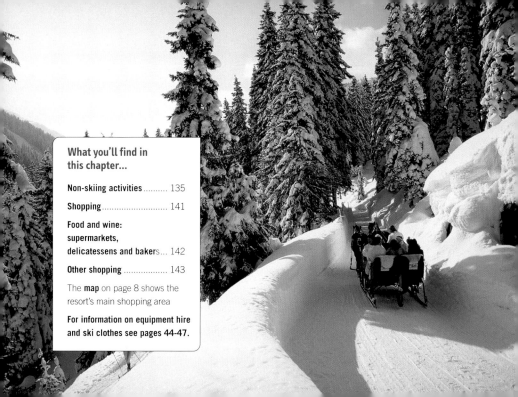

What you'll find in this chapter...

The **map** on page 8 shows the
resort's main shopping area

For information on equipment hire
and ski clothes see pages 44-47.

Activities in St Anton are so focused on the mountain that it isn't an obvious choice for non-skiers. However, if the snow is falling too heavily, or has stopped altogether, there's more than enough to keep you busy.

The ARLBERG-well.com centre

One of the resort's greatest assets is the ARLBERG-well-com building – the sports centre at the base of the piste, near the Fang and Mulden lifts (see map on page 8). Built in 2001 for the World Alpine Skiing Championships, the steel and timber building adds a pleasingly modern slant to the resort. We know people who come to St Anton just to go here! It's well worth a visit and many of the activities are based here. See www.arlberg-well.com or telephone 05446 4001 for more details.

Curling	6-10pm, renting a curling alley for two hours (for a party of four) costs €30, additional people €4 each. Give it a try!
Gym	10am-10pm, €8 (multiple-visit reductions available).
Ice skating	2-6pm, €3 (children €2), skate rental €4 (children €2). Small outdoor rink.

The ARLBERG-well.com centre

Massage	Excellent massages (€46 an hour) are available.
Sauna and steam room	2-10pm (from 11am in bad weather), sauna and wellness pass (which includes access to the swimming pool) €15.50 (reduced to €12.50 after 7pm), towel rental €3 (plus €20 refundable deposit), solarium €7.50. A hot sauna, biosauna (the slightly cooler option!) and stunning steam room are guaranteed to leave you relaxed as long as you are comfortable with the nudity policy enforced in the mixed sauna area and steam room. The changing rooms are also mixed but you can use the separate cubicles for privacy. Leave the slopes a little early if you want a quieter experience.
Swimming	10am-10pm, €10.50 (children €8/4, depending on age), €7.50 after 7pm (children €5/3), weekly and season tickets available, towel hire €3 (plus €20 refundable deposit). Three fantastic swimming pools (indoor, outdoor and one for kids) and various whirlpools. Well worth a visit for the joy of swimming in the snow.

Beauty, massage and spas

Dr Helene Mall

Dorfstrasse 27, opposite the Nah & Frisch supermarket, 0664 2414 997.

Medical massage, reflexology and acupuncture.

Hotel Alte Post

Dorfstrasse 11 (western end), next to Sparkasse bank, 9am-9pm, 05446 2553-0, www.hotel-alte-post.at. From €13.

This cosy 4-star hotel in the centre of the village has an indoor pool, hot tub and sauna which non-residents can use. Various beauty treatments and massages are also available. When the hotel is full, use of the spa by non-guests may be restricted - ask at the hotel reception for details.

Hotel Schwarzer Adler

Dorfstrasse 35, 9am-8pm, 05446 2244-0, www.schwarzeradler.com.

Another 4-star hotel in the centre of town. Although the swimming pool and sauna are for hotel guests only, a wide range of beauty treatment and massages are available for non-residents. See their website for full details.

Many of the resort's other hotels allow non-guests to use their spa/sauna, depending on how busy they are. Ask at reception for details.

Cross-country skiing

See page 37.

Day trips

If you have a free day and feel like seeing a little more of Austria, then the university town of Innsbruck (www.innsbruck-tourismus.com) is just over an hour away. There are several trains a day; you can pick up a timetable from the tourist office or train station. Alternatively, the bus journey to Lech takes about 35 minutes (page 162). It's a pretty resort with some good shops and cafés.

Horse-drawn sleigh rides

Martin Tschol, 05446 2380, email: haus.tschol@arlberg.com.
Sleigh rides in the Verwall Valley.

Internet access

Mailbox

Dorfstrasse 54, on the right-hand side as you head down the street

away from the tourist office
(shortly after the Sport Hotel),
8.30am–8.30pm, 05446 2119,
www.mail-box.at, €0.20 per minute
(season rates available).

Plenty of computers (German keyboards) and a friendly atmosphere. Hot spots, printers and scanners available. There is also a big notice board with local news and job advertisements.

Museum
Rudi-Matt-Weg 10, from the roundabout at the western end of the village walk up Alte Arlbergstrasse and follow signs to the Museum up a winding path, 3-6pm (closed Mondays), 05446 2475.

The Ski Museum covers the history of the Arlberg, skiing and Hannes Schneider. Housed in a beautiful mansion just above the centre of the resort, it's worth a visit, particularly if you plan to enjoy a meal at the good formal restaurant in the same building (page 97).

Paragliding *(Paragleiten)*
Simon Penz, Flight Connection Arlberg, 0664 1415166, www.fca.at (German version only).

Tandem paragliding from Kapall (2300m) to St Anton is particularly popular.

Shopping
See page 141.

Tennis/squash
Bahnhofstrasse 1, near the train station, 05446 2625 for reservations.

Three indoor tennis courts and a squash court.

Tobogganing *(Rodel)*
You'll see the Gampen toboggan run marked in yellow on your piste map, at the top of Nassereinbahn. You can hire a rodel (around €7 plus €20 deposit from most sports shops), take the gondola up and toboggan down. The run - which can get busy and fast! - is open late on Tuesday and Thursday evenings but your lift pass does not cover the gondola ride after 4.30pm. Tickets are €9 one-way (€4.50 for children), €15 evening ticket (€7.50 for children). You can stop part-way down the run to eat at the rustic Rodelalm (page 98).

Shopping

Don't worry about forgetting essentials as St Anton has a good selection of shops, although prices are higher than at home. As you would expect, most of the shops are clustered around the centre (near the tourist office) and along Dorfstrasse, particularly the pedestrian zone. In Nasserein the shopping is more limited but is usually sufficient for any essentials you might need (including equipment hire).

Opening hours

Unless stated otherwise, shops are open from about 8.30am to 7pm. Quite a few close for two or three hours at lunchtime (although they may stay open right through at weekends). Hours can vary a little depending on weather and busy periods – if it's essential phone ahead to check.

Ski clothing and equipment
See page 44.

Food and wine
There are two main supermarkets on Dorfstrasse. As always, the prices are higher in resort than further down the mountain.

You can buy wine from the supermarkets and delis, as well as at the petrol station.

Nah & Frisch
T: 05446 3581
Dorfstrasse, on the right-hand side of the road as you head away from the centre towards Nasserein,
Monday to Saturday: 7.30am-6.30pm, Sunday: 2-6pm.

Good selection of pretty much everything (they even sell chocolate skis!) even more so this season as the shop has been fully refurbished over the summer to include a bigger deli and a separate 'vinotech' wine area. Nearby (on the opposite side of the road) there is an upmarket deli, Schnäppchen, where you can buy local delicacies to take home for yourself or as gifts.

Spar
Dorfstrasse, on the right-hand side of the road as you head away from the centre towards Nasserein, Monday to Saturday: 7am-9pm, Sunday: 10am-9pm, 05446 22020.

Varied general selection including a good butcher.

Bakery
Alberger Dorfbackerie
Dorfstrasse, on the left-hand side of the road as you head away from the centre towards Nasserein, almost opposite Nah & Frisch supermarket. Good sandwiches, cakes and other picnic food. They also have a few tables and it's a friendly place to have a sandwich (€2-3) and some coffee or hot chocolate. Opening hours vary throughout the season but it opens early so you can pick up bread and croissants or have a simple breakfast.

Newsagents and tobacconists.

There is a cigarette machine outside Nah & Frisch supermarket. Cigarettes are sold in supermarkets and vending machines, not in bars.

Presse

Turn right off Dorfstrasse (heading towards Nasserein from the centre of the village) just before the Sport Hotel. The newsagent is almost opposite the chemist.

Bücher-Schreibwaren-Foto-Spiele

Dorfstrasse, in the pedestrian zone (western end), next to Raiffeisenbank .
Useful shop selling a good selection of English books and newspapers along with specialist skiing/snowboarding

books, toys and games. Maps and stationery are also available.

Pharmacy
Arlberg-Apotheke

Turn right off Dorfstrasse (heading in the direction of Nasserein from the centre of the village) just before the Sport Hotel. The pharmacy is a short way down, opposite Scotty's

bar, Monday to Friday: 8am-12pm, 2-6.30pm, Saturday: 8am-12pm, 2-6pm, Sunday: 9am-12pm, 2-6pm, 05446 2061.

A photo developing service is also available.

Photography

You can get your photos developed at the pharmacy or the Post Office.

Skiing with **children**... dream or nightmare? With a little planning, it can be your best ski holiday ever. Read this chapter for the low down.

**What you'll find in
this chapter...**

With a little planning before you arrive, skiing can be a fantastic family holiday. Although St Anton's reputation is primarily built on adult pursuits it does have real appeal for families.

Children are warmly welcomed and there are specific areas where they can enjoy learning to ski, most notably on Gampen (Kindlisfeld and Kinderpark), Nasserein and Rendl. In addition, the ski schools have numerous classes and supervised play times for children. And once skiing is over for the day there are fantastic activities, particularly for slightly older children, such as the toboggan run in Nasserein and swimming in the outdoor pool at the Well.com centre.

If your children are beginners and you want to ski further afield with them, try Zürs and Lech (suitable areas are marked on the piste map with a snowman symbol). Both villages can be reached by Post Bus (page 162). Sonnenkopf is a popular family resort although it's harder to get to (page 30). Depending on what sort of lift pass you have, you may need to extend it to visit these areas; check when buying the pass or at any of the lift pass offices.

Accommodation

If you need childcare, it's far easier to organise if you book your holiday through a tour operator as they will usually have their own arrangements in place. Although the tourist office can provide details of local babysitters you will need to check their experience and credentials yourself. St Anton does not have the English-nanny facilities that some French resorts offer to independent travellers. The other option is to enrol your kids in the international ski schools (page 152).

Your accommodation options all have pros and cons. Children love the social interaction of chalets and hotels and childcare costs can be shared. On the other hand, self-catering arrangements are more flexible (particularly at meal times). If you have young children, being close to the slopes, a bus stop or ski lockers is particularly important if you want to avoid having to carry their skis everywhere for them! The best area to stay is probably the suburb of Nasserein (page 13) as it is close to the nursery slopes and tends to be more peaceful than the centre of the resort. It also has a good selection of family restaurants.

Children's checklist
When booking your holiday, there are a number of questions you may want to ask:

- Are there price reductions or free places available for children?
- Are paraphernalia like cots, high chairs, children's cutlery, buggies and baby monitors provided? If not, can they be bought/hired nearby?
- Does the company offer a nappy-buying service or will you have to bring/buy your own?
- Can extra beds be added into the parents' room?
- Are any other children booked into the chalet? How old are they?
- Are the children's rooms located away from communal areas (which can be noisy until late)?
- Are there baths available (some accommodation only has showers)?
- Have they had complaints in the past about sound proofing in the bedrooms? Quite a few people comment on this and it can be stressful being kept awake by children in the next door room - or feeling guilty about keeping everyone else up.
- Does the company provide its own nannies and/or babysitters? What qualifications do they have and what is the adult to child ratio?
- If childcare isn't provided, can they recommend local carers/facilities?
- Can the company pre-book ski school?
- Can high tea be arranged for children? Are they given different food?
- Is it a long walk to the slopes/nearest bus stop? If so, does the company provide a shuttle bus or lockers near the slopes?

Child-friendly tour operators

Many chalet companies and some hotels in St Anton either offer crèches and nannies for your little ones, or they can arrange them for you. However, facilities tend to be limited, so make sure you reserve them when making your booking. The companies listed below are well-known for their focus on families. For further details of the services offered see maddogski.com.

Esprit:
W: www.esprit-holidays.co.uk
T: 01252 618300

Inghams:
W: www.inghams.co.uk
T: 020 8780 4433

Mark Warner:
W: www.markwarner.co.uk
T: 0870 770 4228

Scott Dunn:
W: www.scottdunn.com
T: 020 8682 5050

Ski Val:
W: www.skival.co.uk
T: 0870 746 3030

Lift passes

Depending on the ski school class you book, lift passes may be included in the cost of instruction, so check when making your reservation.

For general information on passes, as well as where to buy them see page 37. If you are intending to buy a reduced-rate pass then you will need to provide ID (without photo for children up to 1.5m tall). Unusually, the ski-pass reductions are based on the year in which the purchaser was born, rather than their age at the time of purchase. An overview of the main concessions for kids are set out below (for full details see www.skiarlberg.at):

- 'Snowman' tickets for children born in 1999 and after (€10 for the season)
- Reduced rates for children born 1991 to 1998 (ie aged approximately 8 to 15). A six-day pass in the high season costs €116
- Reduced rates for teenagers born 1987 to 1990 (ie aged

149

approximately 16 to 19). A six-day pass in the high season costs €167

Childcare

If your accommodation owner does not offer childcare then we recommend that you make arrangements before you arrive in St Anton. Although competition for facilities isn't as extreme as in some of the larger resorts, it's still sensible to book ahead during busy periods – or at least check to see if it is necessary to do so. Both of the kindergartens below are run by ski schools, which have arrangements for children aged around two-and-a-half upwards.

Kinderwelt ('Children's World')

Run by the Skischule Arlberg, *05446 2526 (main office; opposite* *the Gampen 4-person chairlift),* *05446 273810 (Nasserein),* *www.skischoolarlberg.com.*

Kinderwelt is the resort's main international children's group. Children aged five and older can attend ski classes (see ski schools below). For younger children there are the following options:

1. Ski-kindergarten: non-skiing supervision for children aged above two-and-a-half (they must be out of nappies!). Five days costs €187.
2. Mini special: for children aged three to five years who have never skied before. This isn't formal ski school as such, but rather a course to familiarise

children with being on skis. Classes revolve around having fun in the snow. Maximum six children per group. Five days (four hours per day) costs €187. There is a try-out day on Sundays from 1pm (€28).

For further information and options (including lunchtime supervision) see their website.

Kiki Club

Run by the Skischule St Anton, *based next to the Well.com centre,* *05446 3563, www.skistanton.com.*

As both ski schools are incorporated, facilities and prices are similar to those outlined for Kinderwelt above. See their website for further details.

Ski school

Generally, children can start skiing from around aged four. The stronger they are, the easier they tend to pick it up and the more fun they will have, so although starting younger is possible, older may be preferable. Very young children (aged three to six) may only have the energy to do half a day on the slopes. The rest of the time might be better spent playing in the snow, or back in the resort (see suggested activities on page 154).

Many instructors teach children to ski through a series of games, analogies, copying and races, so they pick up new skills without too much technical information. Kids may talk about how they were making 'chips' and not 'pizza' – this just means that they are moving into parallels instead of snowplough – or being 'tall as a house' and 'small as a mouse', which is a useful way to encourage children to move up at the start of the turn and down at the end.

Skiing is all about having fun, so don't worry too much about the progress of very young children. If your child is having a good time, they'll be hooked for life and the technical improvement will come. If you have any worries, speak to the instructor.

Groups vs private lessons

It used to be that in order for children to get the individual attention they need to progress technically, private lessons were the only option. However, ski schools now offer smaller group sizes for children (between five and 10 members) where the children can enjoy the social side of being in a class but still receive individual instruction. Kids love the interaction with other children that groups offer, so this can be the ideal environment to learn in. With encouragement and friendly competition, many children progress quickly.

In St Anton children aged five and over can go to ski school. If your holiday has been arranged through a tour operator, check with them before booking as they may have arrangements in place with one of the schools.

Both schools in St Anton are Austrian-run, so request an English-speaking instructor when making your booking. If you are also taking lessons, check where your meeting point is in relation to your children's so that you can be on hand to drop them off and collect them. For full details of the schools see page 42.

Skischule Arlberg

Classes are supplemented by additional extras including a treasure hunt, mountain rally and weekly races. Five days' tuition (four hours a day) costs €187. See www.skischoolarlberg.com for details.

Skischule St Anton

Skischule St Anton offers similar services for children at the same price. See www.skistanton.com for details.

First day at ski school checklist

- Write your mobile or other contact number on a piece of paper and place it in your child's coat pocket in case you are needed urgently
- Plenty of high factor sun cream (water resistant and at least 30 SPF) is essential. Put the tube in their pocket so they can top up throughout the day
- Most experts recommend that children should ski with helmets. You can hire these in resort
- Younger eyes are more sensitive so it is important to make kids wear good quality sunglasses or goggles all the time. If you only plan to buy one or the other, buy goggles
- Take time to find gloves or mittens that your child can take on and off easily by themselves; they'll have to do this numerous times throughout the day!
- A small rucksack is useful for slightly older kids for carrying drinks, snacks and sun cream
- Children lose body heat faster than adults so make sure they are wrapped up warmly
- If you are booking younger children into ski school, remember to give them a drink and snack for the mid-lesson break (or money to buy them). Check with the ski school if you are unsure
- Talk to the instructor before the first lesson as any information will be useful (for example, do they get tired easily/hate drag lifts/have any allergies or other medical considerations)

and distraction and provides many of the activities. You will find it in the centre of the resort, between the Fang and Mulden lifts.

- Even if your children are not in ski school, you will probably find it helpful to mark clothes, skis and helmets with their name as things are often thrown into a big bundle in the rush to get inside at break or lunch time! If you don't have any labels for skis and helmets, write on sticking plasters
- If possible buy gloves and hats that can be attached to your child; otherwise they go missing endlessly...
- Complete beginners (especially the little ones) will probably not need to take poles to their ski

lessons, at least for the first few days – check with your ski school
- You may not need to buy a ski pass for the first few days, or the pass may be included in the cost of lessons. Again, check when booking

Children's activities

Many of the suggestions in **Other things to do** (page 135) are also suitable for children, especially those who are a little older. St Anton's modern sport centre, ARLBERG-well.com (page 135), is a brilliant source of entertainment

Ice skating

Outside the Well.com centre.
See page 135.

Tobogganing

You can buy bum boards for a few euros in lots of shops around the resort and play around on the gentle slopes close to the village centre once the lifts are closed.

There's an exhilarating time to be had on the four-kilometre toboggan run (Rodel) which begins at Gampen and goes down to Nasserein – you'll see it marked on the piste map in yellow. Be warned that it does get quite competitive as people race one another, particularly on Tuesday and Thursday evenings when it is often busy, so it's probably more suitable for teenagers than little ones. The run has a descent of 509m and takes about 15 minutes to complete. For more details see page 140.

Swimming

The Well.com centre has an indoor and (more excitingly) a heated outdoor pool, along with whirlpools of various sizes. Family rates available. See page 136.

Restaurants

Restaurants in resort and on the mountain are used to children and generally go out of their way to

welcome them. Most offer simple dishes that children can enjoy and some have children's menus or portions. Our restaurant reviews have more detail but we particularly recommend these places.

Anton restaurant
T: 05446 2408

Near Galzigbahn, 11am-11pm. Relaxed friendly café with separate children's play area.

The menu has various soups, salads and pastas. Small portions available for kids. Page 87.

Aquila
T: 05446 2217

Dorfstrasse, near the Spar supermarket, 6-10pm.

More of a café than a restaurant. The food is average but service is quick, prices are reasonable and there is plenty of space. Good kids' meals include spaghetti, nuggets and wiener schnitzel. Refurbished for the 2006/7 season. Page 88.

Hax'n Stub'n
T: 05446 3870

Near the roundabout at the west end of town, a minute's walk from Galzigbahn, 10am-8pm, (reservations for after 7pm only).

Conveniently situated near the slopes, this family-run restaurant serves good filling food. They're used to kids as ski school classes go there for lunch! Very busy between 1-2pm. Page 93.

Maximilian
T: 05446 42675

Dorfstrasse, further down from Spar (on the opposite side of the road, in the direction of Nasserein), 11am-11pm.

If your children are happy with Austrian food this is a popular choice as it's friendly and near lots of hotels at the eastern end of the resort. Soups, baked potatoes and steaks can be found amongst some more elaborate dishes. Crayons are thoughtfully provided to keep the kids occupied. Page 96.

Pizza Pomodoro
T: 05446 3333

Next to Platzl bar on the main street (west end), 6-10.30pm, no reservations.

The most popular pizza restaurant in town offers, as you would expect, a wide choice of pizzas plus daily specials and homemade lasagne. If you're with children, be warned that it can get quite rowdy later on! Good alternatives are San Antonio in Nasserein (page 99) or Floriani on Alte Arlbergstrasse (page 92). Page 97.

Mountain restaurants

Most of the mountain restaurants will do all they can to accommodate families. The main problem you will encounter are lunchtime queues. Try to eat early (12.30pm or before) or go to self-service restaurants where you will hopefully get your food quicker. Another option is to buy food in resort (see page 142) and enjoy a panoramic picnic.

Reviews of all mountain restaurants in the ski area start on page 115 but these are our favourites if you have little ones with you (all have access for skiers and pedestrians):

Galzig and Kandahar

T: 05446 2352501

*At the top of Galzigbahn,
8.30am-4.15pm.*

These restaurants may not provide
the most serene environment, but
are convenient for lift access and
popular with families as there's lots
of space. Self-service with a choice
of salad bar, pasta, pizza and simple
meat dishes. Prices are average. If
you want something more refined,
you can eat in the attached Verwall
Stube restaurant page 121.

Rendl Beach

T: 05446 2352550

*At the top of the Rendl gondola,
9am-4pm.*

Sun-spot that draws the crowds;
deckchairs, volley ball and live
music. When there's enough snow,
you'll find a giant snowman here.
The food (stir-fries, a good salad bar,
huge helpings of pasta) is basic but
reliable and prices are reasonable.
The self-service queues do build up
at peak hours so arrive early if you
can. There are easy blue runs near
the restaurant. Page 125.

Valluga

T: 05446 2352520

*At the top of Valluga I cablecar, 9am-
3.45pm (erratic opening hours;
access restricted in bad weather).*

The spectacular view from the top
is worth the trip for older kids (the
altitude, 2650m, might be too
much for some younger ones). The
menu is based on classic Austrian
staples such as schnitzel, toasts
and knödel soup. Page 127.

Shopping

Supermarkets stock babyfood and
formula but if you have any
favourite products it's best to bring
them with you. Most ski shops
stock children's sizes too so it's
easy to replace any lost items.
Bücher-Schreibwaren-Foto-Spiele,
the general shop near the western
end of Dorfstrasse (next to
Raiffeisenbank) has a selection of
toys and games.

The list – sounds boring but it has all the important information that you don't need till you need it...

Telephone numbers include local codes (page 5). From the UK dial '00 43' and then drop the first '0'

Austrian mobile telephone numbers begin with '06'

Street names coincide with those shown on the tourist office maps (we also use them on our maps). We use local landmarks as points of reference (page 8)

Banks, bureau de change and cashpoints

There are numerous banks and cashpoints, particularly along Dorfstrasse. Opening hours shown are Monday to Friday.

Raiffeisenbank

Next to the English bookshop on Dorfstrasse (western end of the village), 8am-12pm, 2-5pm.

Reisebank

On the roundabout near the tourist office, 9am-2pm, 3-6.15pm. Closed Wednesdays. Bureau de change and Western Union services available.

Sparkasse

Near Hotel Alte Post on Dorfstrasse, 8.30am-12pm, 2-4.30pm.

Sporthotel

On Dorfstrasse. There is a cashpoint machine outside the hotel.

Volksbank

Next to the Sport Hotel on Dorfstrasse, 8am-12pm, 2-5pm.

British Consulate

For lost passports contact the British Consulate in Innsbruck: Monday to Friday: 9am-12pm.
T: 0512 588320
F: 0512 579973-8
Out of hours number:
T: 0512 579973.
Kaiserjägerstrasse 1/Top B9, 6020 Innsbruck

Buses

In resort

Free 'ski buses' run between St Anton and its outlying suburbs. Whilst these are fairly frequent, picking up a timetable (*Fahrplan*) from the tourist office will reduce time hanging around in the cold. Times for the first and last buses vary from route to route but they tend to start between 7.30-8.30am and finish around 5.30-6.30pm.

The main bus terminal ('Terminal West' on timetables) is at the western end of town, just off the roundabout near the tourist office (see map on page 8). All of the ski buses start and finish here. Other bus stops throughout the resort are indicated by a yellow post with 'H' at the top (*Halt* means 'stop'). Times and

The ski bus has five main routes. The number and destination are marked on the front of the bus:

Line	Destination	Approximate travel time from Terminal West to furthest bus stop	Comment
1 (Blue)	Rendl	3 minutes	You can catch this bus either from Terminal West or the Anton café near Galzigbahn. It runs very frequently
2 (Green)	St Jakob	25 minutes	St Jakob is the suburb at the far eastern end of the village (page 13)
3 (Red)	Mooserkreuz	7 minutes	Stops at Rendl, then continues along the Arlberg Pass to the Mooserkreuz (where you can exit for the Krazy Kangaruh, Taps and Mooserwirt – see page 124), then back to the village via Alte Arlbergstrasse
4 (Purple)	Nasserein	10 minutes	Nasserein is the suburb at the eastern end of town, around Nassereinbahn (page 13)
5 (Yellow)	Untergand	10 minutes	Heads beyond St Jakob, along the main road past M-Preis supermarket. This route avoids the village so is faster than Line 2

161

directions are displayed at the bus stops.

There is also a night bus *(Nachtbus)* in St Anton which operates from mid-December to mid-April. It is limited to two routes; Galzigbahn to St Jakob and Galzigbahn to Oberdorf (via Alte Arlbergstrasse). Buses run every hour from around 7pm until 2am. Tickets cost €3.50.

During peak periods the buses can get crowded. If you don't want to rely on them, rent your equipment from a hire shop that offers overnight storage (page 44) so you can walk back to your accommodation more easily. Details of taxi services are given on page 169.

Buses to other resorts

If you want to travel to other resorts by bus then you will need to use the commercial bus line, Post Bus. These buses are usually yellow (except when they're white!) and are clearly marked 'Post Bus'. You can pick up a bus timetable from the tourist office. As with the ski bus, they leave from Terminal West.

To Lech:

The journey from St Anton to Lech costs €3.60 one-way and takes about 35 minutes. If you are planning to catch the bus back to St Anton from Lech/Zürs at the end of the day, remember that you will need to get the Post Bus, as Lech's local bus will only take you as far as Alpe Rauz. Buses to St Anton go every half hour or so from Lech and Zürs, with the last one leaving around 5pm.

An alternative route to Zürs and Lech is to ski to Alpe Rauz from St Anton, via the wonderfully long 17 (Valfagehr). At the bottom of the run you will find the bus terminal next to the car park (usefully marked with a 'P' on your piste map); it's about two minutes' walk from where you clip out of your skis. From there you can catch the free ski bus which runs to Zürs and Lech or (if you don't mind paying) you can take the Post Bus.

If you have been skiing in Lech and end up in Alpe Rauz then you can catch the Post Bus back to St Anton. It costs €2.60

one way and takes about 15 minutes.

Buses to the airport
For the latest information on getting to and from airports by bus or private transfer see maddogski.com.

Car hire
For information on car hire from airports see page 22.

If you want to hire a car whilst in St Anton they're best booked in advance from Avis (which operates from the Shell garage). This can be done online at www.avis.at or call 05446 3466.

Car parks
The centre of the resort is pretty much closed to traffic however there are car parks dotted around (about 2000 spaces in all). The main ones can be found at Rendl and Nassereinbahn. The price is around €7 per day per car.

Cashpoints
See banks page 159.

Churches
The tourist office has up-to-date information and times for church services.

Cinema
Films are shown in the Valluga Saal, above the tourist office, on occasional evenings throughout the winter. Check with the tourist office for details.

Credit cards
Credit cards (except American Express) and especially debit cards (EC-cards) are widely accepted in resort but less so in the mountain restaurants. When paying by card you'll need a PIN number.

Dentist (*Zahnarzt*)
Dr Hugo Juen, Im Gries 22, near the pharmacy, 05446 2070.

Doctor (*Ärzte*)
Dr Knierzinger
Based in the medical centre in the precinct near the tourist office, Monday to Friday 7.30-10.30am, 05446 2828.

Dr Markus Sprenger

Marketstrasse 26, near the church at the eastern end of town, 05446 3200.

General practitioner, sports injuries and physiotherapy.

Electricity

Austria operates on a 220 volts system but UK appliances should work with an adaptor (the two round pin type).

Emergency numbers

Fire Brigade 122
Medical Emergency 144
Police 133 (local police 05446 236213)
European Emergency Services 112

The environment

There is always a tremendous amount of rubbish on the slopes when the snow melts – don't add to it! A single cigarette butt contains 4,000 toxic substances and can pollute up to 1.3 m³ of snow – under any one chairlift there could be up to 30,000 butts.

How long does rubbish last?
Plastic bottle: 100 - 1000 years
Aluminium cans: 100 – 500 years
Cigarette stubs: 2 – 7 years
Fruit peel: 3 days – 6 months
Sweet wrappers: 100 – 450 years

Source: www.mountain-riders.org

The Ski Club of Great Britain runs a campaign aimed at safeguarding the environment and the long-term future of skiing.
See www.respectthemountain.com for details.

St Anton are doing their part by repairing erosion damage on the mountain, along with planting and draining programmes. Resorts in the Tyrol don't use chemicals in their artificial snow, just pure water.

Ski rescue service

St Anton/St Christoph

T: 05446 2352223

Stuben

T: 05582 550

Lech/Oberlech/Zürs

T: 05583 2855

It's a good idea to programme the ski rescue service numbers into your mobile phone at the beginning of your holiday. The numbers can also be found on the back of the piste map.

Garages

There is a Shell garage at the eastern entrance of the resort from the main road which can also arrange car hire (page 163).

For mechanical work contact KFZ Haid, Nassereinerstrasse 53, 05446 2080.

Hairdresser (*Friseur*)

Both places listed below are small local salons:

Team Anita

Markstrasse 22 (behind the church at the east end of town, near the medical centre), 05446 30383.

Friseursalon Peter

Dorfstrasse, next to the Mailbox internet café, Tuesday, Wednesday and Friday: 8am-7pm, Thursday: 9am-8pm, Saturday: 8am-3pm, 05446 30156.
New for the 2006/7 season.

Health

A few tips to keep you healthy on holiday:

- the sun is much stronger at altitude – make sure you wear sun cream, even on overcast days (don't forget under your chin where the snow reflects the sun!)
- you need to drink at least three times as much water to keep hydrated at altitude – more if you are topping up with wine and beer! Your muscles are the first part of your body to dehydrate so you'll suffer less aches and pains if you keep hydrated
- good sunglasses are a must to prevent watering eyes and snow blindness

- lip salve with a high sun-
protection factor will prevent
unattractive chapped lips!

Hospital
Hospital Zams, Sanatoriumstrasse
43, 6511 Zams, 05442 6000.
30km from St Anton.

Internet
See page 138.

Language
Although many of the people
working in shops and restaurants
speak English, a little German goes
a long way. Don't be discouraged
if you don't understand their
response as some of the local
vocabulary may vary slightly to
standard German or Austrian.

Useful words and phrases:	
Hello	Guten Tag
Goodbye	Auf Wiedersehen
How are you?	Wie geht's (dir)? (informal) Wie geht es Ihnen? (polite)
Please	Bitte
Thank you	Danke
Excuse me/sorry	Entschuldigen Sie bitte
How much..?	Wie viel kostet…?
The bill please	Bitte/zahlen
Jug of tap water	Leitungswassers
Snowboard	Snowboard
Skis	Ski
Binding	Bindung
Ski/boarding boots	Skichuhe/Snowboard Schuhe
Ski poles	Stöcke
Lift pass	Skipass/Liftpass
I am lost	Ich habe mich verlaufen
Where is the nearest lift? bar?	Wo ist die näheste Lift? Snipper?
Help!	Hilfe!
Watch out!	VorSieht!

- Nouns in German all start with a capital letter eg Fahrplan (bus timetable)
- Nouns also start with either der (m), die (f) or das (n) to signify gender. Plurals always begin with die
- German is quite easy to read since there are many similar sounds as in English. However, you will come across certain vowels that carry two dots above them, the umlaut, that signifies a joining of the letter 'e' and a different sound. They are pronounced in the following way:

Ä (ae) – sounds like 'air' eg Äpfel (apple); Ü (ue) – sounds like 'oo' eg glück (luck); Ö (oe) - sounds like 'ur' eg schön (beautiful). Note: you can replace the umlaut with the letter 'e' eg Aepfel. This is considered just as correct
- People generally refer to themselves by their surname, so use this if you have reserved a restaurant or hotel eg Mein Name ist Jones (my name is Jones)
- Whilst German is the main language in Austria, there will be some dialectic differences compared to Switzerland and Germany. These are mostly associated with greetings and farewells

Lost and found *(Fundamt)*
Town Hall, Dorfstrasse 46, Monday to Thursday: 8am-12pm, 1pm-5pm, Friday: 8am-12pm, 05446 23620.

If you lose your ski pass, ask at the nearest lift-pass office to see if it has been handed in and check at the Lost and Found. The general principle is that lift passes will not be replaced however it is worth holding onto your lift pass receipt in case of loss, as in certain circumstances it may be possible to negotiate a replacement.

Massage
See page 138.

Meeting rooms
You can hire meeting rooms at the Well.com sport centre, 05446 4001, www.arlberg-well.com. Contact the centre for details.

Money
All prices in this book are given in

euro unless indicated otherwise, and based on the 2005/6 season. You can find up-to-date exchange rates at www.xe.com. See also cashpoints (page 159) and credit cards (page 163).

Physiotherapist

Dr Josef Knierzinger, Arlberg Day Clinic, Sollederweg 5, 05446 42666, www.tagesklinik-arlberg.at. See also massage (page 138).

Police (*Polizei*)

Dorfstrasse, opposite Hotel Post and the Piccadilly, 05446 236213.

There is another police station at Kirchgasse 2, in the eastern end of the village, behind the church, 05446 2237.

Post Office (*Postamt*)

Postplatz 2, walk down Dorfstrasse in the direction of Nasserein, turning right just before Parfumerie Bano. At the junction follow signs to the Post Office. Monday to Friday 8am-12pm, 2-5.30pm, 05446 3380.

There are several public telephones outside the Post Office and their shop also sells stationery, film and mobile phones.

Most shops selling postcards will also sell stamps to the UK. There are yellow post boxes around the resort. Post should take two to four days to get to the UK.

Safety

Ski resorts are traditionally a safe

place to holiday. The few crimes there are usually involve theft so ensure you keep your belongings with you in bars and also keep your accommodation locked at all times.

To protect your skis from theft, you should get into the habit of swapping skis with your companions so you leave mismatched pairs outside restaurants and bars. Some restaurants have ski checks that you can use for a small charge.

Taxis

Taxis aren't cheap (particularly at night) but, if there is a group of you, they are an easy way to get around. Most taxi drivers speak at least some English. You'll find taxi ranks outside the train station and at the western end of town near the Anton hotel/restaurant. Alternatively, call one of the taxi companies to collect you:

Arlberg Car	05446 3730
Taxi Harry	05446 2315
Taxi Isepponi	05446 2275/2179
Taxi Lami	05446 2806
Tyroltours	05446 3361

From St Anton:

To	Daytime fare (€)	Evening fare (€)
St Christoph	20	30
Lech	46	69
Stuben	39	59
Zürs	39	59

Telephones

See page 5.

Time

Austrian time is GMT +1 hour.

Tipping

Restaurants and bars: people leave what they want; around 10% is standard

Instructors: if you enjoyed your week of lessons, tip your instructor €10-15 each

Chalet hosts: most survive the season on next to nothing. If yours makes a positive difference to your holiday, they will certainly not be offended by a cash gift at the end of the week! Tip at least €10-15 per adult guest; more for exceptional service or in luxury chalets.

Toilets (*Toiletten*)

Galzigbahn base station is one of the few places in the village to have public toilets. On the mountain there are public toilets at the main cable car stations.

Tourist office

The tourist office is at the west end of the village, slightly set back from the roundabout and near Surfer's Paradise, Monday to Friday: 8.30am-7pm, Saturday: 9am-6pm, Sunday: 9am-12pm, 2-5pm, 05446 22690, www.stantonamarlberg.com.

Staff are very helpful and speak excellent English. As well as the general information you'd expect, you can get bus timetables (for both the free ski bus and the Post Bus), village maps and piste maps.

The tourist office has detailed information about the resort's hotels and guest houses on their website. If you arrive in resort without somewhere to stay, they also have an accommodation service: turn left out of the office and left again and you will see a display of hotels and guesthouses, with information on availability.

Websites and contact numbers for tourist offices in the region are as follows:

www.lech.at
T: 05583 21610

www.zuers.at
T: 05583 2245

www.stuben.com
T: 05582 399

www.stantonamarlberg.com

T: 05446 22690

(St Christoph and St Anton share a tourist office)

www.sonnenkopf.com

T: 05582 2920

Trains

See page 22.

Weather

Generally you can expect January and February to be colder than March and April. December is less snow sure but correspondingly cheaper, except around Christmas and New Year.

The following provide current weather forecasts:

- **maddogski.com** weather forecasts and webcams
- **www.snow-forecast.com** three and six-day weather forecasts
- **www.stantonamarlberg.com** the tourist office website has a weather section with a five-day forecast
- **www.skiarlberg.at** information on weather, lifts, slopes and avalanche risk
- Daily weather information can be found on the two local channels shown in most hotels and chalets ('Panorama-Channel' and 'Arlberg TV')

Index

A

B

C

D

E

And finally...

We would like to thank the following people for their help and support: Susie Aust, Philip Blackwell, Joey Draxl, Nick Funnell, Carrie Hainge at the Ski Club of Great Britain, Laurent Kssis, the St Anton Tourist office (Wilma Himmelfreundpointner, Anna Stefanitsch and Eva-Marie Hüttl), Paul Markham, Sonja Maier, Erica Meredith-Hardy (for her contribution to the **Children** chapter), Janelle Stettler, Carrie Stokes, Nadine Stothard, Ruth and Graham from Piste to Powder, Rexy and Blackie and all those who make St Anton such a great place to be.

Photo credits

TVB St Anton am Arlberg (St Anton tourist office): P2, 9, 14, 16, 17, 19, 23, 27, 68, 73, 114, 122, 132, 137, 139, 141, 143, 144, 147, 149, 151, 154
Divider: About St Anton, On the piste, Other things to do
Arlberger Bergbahnen AG – Piste maps
Emma Hardcastle – P29
Divider: Children
Graham Austick (Piste to Powder) – Front cover
Divider: About Mad Dog

Henry Meredith Hardy – P3
Hospiz.com – P89, 91, 95, 100, 102, 108, 110, 124, 128, 133
Divider: Planning your trip, Food and drink
Kate Whittaker – P47, 81
Oliver Lee – P158, 172
Tory Dean – P24, 33, 39, 62, 76, 161, 168
Divider: The list

Do you know something we don't? Jot down your tips and recommendations and lets us know about them at info@maddogski.com

**Do you know something we don't? Jot down your
tips and recommendations and lets us know about
them at info@maddogski.com**

Do you know something we don't? Jot down your tips and recommendations and lets us know about them at info@maddogski.com

Do you know something we don't? Jot down your tips and recommendations and lets us know about them at info@maddogski.com

Do you know something we don't? Jot down your tips and recommendations and lets us know about them at info@maddogski.com

Do you know something we don't? Jot down your tips and recommendations and lets us know about them at info@maddogski.com

Do you know something we don't? Jot down your tips and recommendations and lets us know about them at info@maddogski.com

Do you know something we don't? Jot down your tips and recommendations and lets us know about them at info@maddogski.com

Do you know something we don't? Jot down your tips and recommendations and lets us know about them at info@maddogski.com

Do you know something we don't? Jot down your tips and recommendations and lets us know about them at info@maddogski.com

Do you know something we don't? Jot down your tips and recommendations and lets us know about them at info@maddogski.com